# Los Angeles

A guide to recent architecture

...

**Dian Phillips-Pulverman with Peter Lloyd**

# Los Angeles

A guide to recent architecture

● ● ● **ellipsis KÖNEMANN**

•••

**Los Angeles: a guide to recent architecture**

CREATED, EDITED AND DESIGNED BY
Ellipsis London Limited
55 Charlotte Road London EC2A 3QT
E MAIL ...@ellipsis.co.uk
www http://www.ellipsis.co.uk/ellipsis
PUBLISHED IN THE UK AND AFRICA BY
Ellipsis London Limited
SERIES EDITOR Tom Neville
SERIES DESIGN Jonathan Moberly
EDITOR Vicky Wilson
LAYOUT Pauline Harrison

COPYRIGHT © 1996 Könemann
Verlagsgesellschaft mbH
Bonner Str. 126, D-50968 Köln
PRODUCTION MANAGER Detlev Schaper
PRINTING AND BINDING Sing Cheong
Printing Ltd
Printed in Hong Kong

ISBN 3 89508 285 6 (Könemann)
ISBN 1 899858 09 1 (Ellipsis)

**Dian Phillips-Pulverman 1994**

# Contents

# Introduction

This guidebook contains descriptions of more than 100 buildings completed in Los Angeles over the last ten years. Many are well known and designed by architects who are, by now, household names. But the book also focuses on less well-known architects as well as the established figures who continue to produce interesting work not much in the public eye as it stands outside the pervading style that has been labelled the 'LA School'.

The image of Los Angeles architecture over the last ten years has been largely shaped by books, magazines and exhibitions that concentrate on this particular body of work, practised by Frank O Gehry, Morphosis, Eric O Moss and Frank D Israel, among others, and a younger generation including Michele Saee, O'Herlihy + Warner and studio bau:ton. The 'LA School' style is characterised most notably by bold, strong buildings with unexpected juxtapositions, disrupted forms that may tilt or be wrenched apart, inventive uses and combinations of basic industrial materials, and detailing that is designed as if it were jewellery.

While the style of these architects' projects has been widely discussed and has contributed to recent debates on deconstruction, buildings pursuing other interests have been less celebrated. Continuing modernist principles can be seen in a number of houses by Pierre Koenig and Raymond Kappe and the 7th Street offices by David Lawrence Gray. Charles Ward's own cloistered house employs a rationalist sensibility with overtones of Barragán. And Charles Moore working with Moore Ruble Yudell on St Matthew's Church and with Urban Innovations Group on the Beverly Hills Civic Center has continued his postmodern tendencies.

With Los Angeles' unifying structure – the freeway system – becoming increasingly clogged due to rapid population growth, the 1990s have seen the start of the city's efforts to replace its vanished public transport system. So far, 4.4 miles of new MetroRail have been completed with five stations connecting Union Station to Westlake/MacArthur Park. Ultimately, by 2001 it should connect to North Hollywood and other subway and light-rail links. Given the size of the Los Angeles sprawl, the success of this limited rail system could depend on areas increasing their density. There are now new mixed-use developments that attempt to accomplish this (see, for example, Venice Renaissance by Johannes van Tilburg).

The last ten years have also seen some rediscovery of Los Angeles' lost tradition of public spaces. The 3rd Street Promenade in Santa Monica – edged to the south by Frank Gehry's Santa Monica Place and Steven Ehrlich's Broadway Deli, and to the north by Hennesey and Ingalls, an art and architecture bookstore with a Morphosis-designed elevation – is constantly packed with people.

Efforts were made to provide spaces that would promote a vibrant public life in the Beverley Hills Civic Center but they have been thwarted by municipal short-sightedness and financial cutbacks. Breathing life back into Los Angeles' oldest public park is the recently completed Pershing Square designed by Ricardo Legorreta and Hanna/Olin. City-Walk at Universal Studios is also very successful and popular, but remains contentious as it raises the question of whether public spaces should be privatised.

Responding to social needs, a number of care-oriented buildings have surfaced. To meet demand for daycare, a clutch of delightful and stimulating pre-schools have been built (see the UCLA Children's Center by the Office of Charles and Elizabeth Lee and the Samuel Goldwyn Children's Center by Solberg + Lowe). Continuing the slow and limited efforts to find affordable housing for the homeless, a number of single-room-

**Los Angeles: a guide to recent architecture**

occupancy hotels have been renovated. And there is now a new SRO hotel, the Simone, by Koning Eizenberg. Also caring for the homeless is Genesis I, a community of semi-domed structures designed by Craig Chamberlain and inspired by Buckminster Fuller.

During these ten years there has been a small number of patrons who are committed to commissioning world-class architects. As a result, they have created new pockets in the city in which distinguished architecture is collected. Charles Oakley, the head of UCLA's campus architects, has, along with Dean Richard Weinstein, brought in many talented architects to build on the UCLA campus (see the MacDonald Medical Research Laboratory by Venturi Scott Brown, the Energy Services Facility by Holt Hinshaw Pfau Jones, and the Towell Library by Hodgetts + Fung). In East Culver City, Frederick Norton Smith is steadily transforming a derelict area of industrial buildings into commercial space that largely caters to people working in creative fields, consistently employing Eric O Moss as his architect. And over in Burbank at the Walt Disney Studios, Michael Eisner has new buildings completed, nearing completion, and on the drawing boards by Michael Graves, Robert M Stern and Venturi Scott Brown, respectively.

Outside of these pockets, the fabric of the city is largely distinguished by the banal – strip malls, low-rise structures and parking lots. Kanner Architects have improved greatly on the strip mall as can be seen in the Montana Collection. With their Kentucky Fried Chicken building, Grinstein Daniels have shown what can be done with a fast-food outlet.

Moving into the next decade, interest seem to be shifting from architecture as object-making towards city building. Stimulated largely by the 1992 riots, this has not yet manifested itself in built form, but it has been evident in the architecture schools, in exhibitions such as *Urban Revisions*

– *Current Projects for the Public Realm* at the Museum of Contemporary Art, and in the efforts of the Design Professionals Coalition, a group of architects who provide *pro bono* design services to communities in need of rehabilitation. But, due for completion in 1996 are the Getty Center by Richard Meier, sited on a mountain top and devoting more than 50,000 square feet to the arts and humanities, and Frank Gehry's Disney Concert Hall. These are the projects that are slated to become Los Angeles' next landmarks.

**Los Angeles: a guide to recent architecture**

**Using this book**

This guide is divided into 12 sections, each defining an area of Los Angeles where there are buildings of interest. Although Los Angeles does have a public transport system, the best way to negotiate the sprawl is by car. The map co-ordinates for the current edition of *The Thomas Guide Los Angeles County Street Guide and Directory* are listed under each entry after the address to guide you to the precise location of the building.

A large proportion of the interesting buildings in Los Angeles are private residences. The owners who have agreed to allow their houses to be included in this guide have done so on the understanding that their non-accessibility is stressed. Please respect their privacy.

## Acknowledgements

I would like to thank all of the architects whose work is included in the guide for generously providing time, information, and images; Peter Lloyd who came to the rescue and wrote a significant portion of the book; photographer Erhard Pfeiffer for taking additional pictures; Frances Anderton who acted repeatedly as a resource and was always generous with opinions and information; Vicky Wilson for editing; Martin Pulverman for supporting, encouraging and pushing; and Tom Neville, who always remained tolerant.
DP August 1994

**Los Angeles: a guide to recent architecture**

# Malibu

Although Ed Niles vehemently rejects the analogy, the Sidley Residence does look like nothing so much as a vessel from outer space. But if not that, then how about a steel praying mantis standing next to a half-buried Ferris wheel? Either way it doesn't look like a house.

The Ferris wheel is a half drum made of steel and glass that contains the entrance, a living area and the kitchen. Another doorway opens on to a swimming pool and patio where token contact is made with the surrounding landscape. From the wheel, a spindly bridge over the driveway leads to the bedrooms, bathrooms and study areas. This part of the house is elevated above the ground by concrete piers and has 'pods' in the shape of quarter circles attached to a central passageway. The pods house small rooms made of curved steel panels with glass walls.

Niles has said that the project is a 'symbol of man separated from or hostile to the natural elements', and with this in mind, the house seems a direct descendant of Archigram's post-apocalyptic architecture of the 1960s. Aspects of both Ron Herron's 'Walking City' and Peter Cook's 'Plug-in City' find expression in this forceful and individual vision. PL

ADDRESS 27929 Winding Way, Malibu 90265
[667–H1]
CLIENT M Sidley
STRUCTURAL ENGINEER Dimitry Vergun
SIZE 4000 square feet (370 square metres)
ACCESS none

Malibu

**Ed Niles 1985**

**Ed Niles 1985**

# Miller Residence

This residence consists of two independent but complementary buildings. Open-plan living spaces, kitchen and bedrooms are located in the main, front house. Behind this, connected by a bridge, is an elliptical tower that contains a studio and additional bedroom. The house faces the ocean, and maximising this view was of prime importance. The clients also requested thorough interior daylighting, while protecting their privacy. This led to the most notable aspect of the house – the extensive use of glass for external walls.

The front elevation is of clear glass. To screen the interior from the side neighbours, the east and west elevations are of translucent glasses – laminated glass and a channel glass more commonly found in Europe. This has created spaces filled with natural light in which the view has become a dominant part of the interior.

Isolating architectural elements and making them objects is a practice used throughout. White plaster ceilings (supported by the exposed steel frame) are separated from the glass curtain walls. The planes of glass also pull away from the solid stairway. Even the internal walls are visually separated from each other through the use of different muted colours.

To gain the ocean view, the living quarters sit 16 feet above grade on top of the garage and stand 35 feet high, allowing the house's sight lines to skim over the roofs across the street. The recent change in Malibu height restrictions means this house could not have been built today.

ADDRESS 26645 Latigo Shore Drive, Malibu 90265 [668–B1]
CLIENTS Mike and Patricia Miller
STRUCTURAL ENGINEER William Koh
SIZE 5400 square feet (500 square metres)
ACCESS none

**Malibu**

**O'Herlihy + Warner Architects 1993**

Malibu

**Somerfield Residence**

Perched on a hillside high above Malibu, this is a house that explores space in a sculptural way. A rectilinear volume is linked to a curved volume that encircles a small open space leading on to a motor court. White plasterwork and strong sunlight give the impression of a seashell or bleached bone smoothed by the ocean. Angled roofs make each internal space an adventure of unexpected forms that flow from one to the other with casual grace. Skylights and unexpected window openings fill the structure with painterly bands of sunlight.

Seen from the foot of the hill, a strongly geometric *brise soleil* standing next to the softer curved form dominates the composition, and though dramatic, it offers little insight into the house's less ostentatious virtues. PL

ADDRESS 24744 Vantage Point Terrace, Malibu 90265 [628–G7]
CLIENT Gil and Ellie Somerfield
STRUCTURAL ENGINEER Kurily Szymanski Tchirkow
SIZE 6500 square feet (600 square metres)
COST $1.25 million
ACCESS none

Malibu

**Goldman/Firth/Boccato Architects 1994**

**'24955 PCH'**

This is an office development that eschews a monolithic form in favour of a village-like feeling. A broken grid of what looks like poured-in-place concrete but is in fact stucco-work creates a ghost façade – the remains of what might have existed. Three storeys high at each end, the structure steps down to an informal courtyard at the heart of the complex. Pavilions faced with green glass, with either arched or angled roof lines, rise up from the apparent solidity of the main structure to create a roofscape of urban complexity. Open spaces in the form of courtyards, balconies and walkways further fragment the building. Careful planting, designed to bring the hillside through the built forms, emphasises the particular character of Malibu, where the ocean meets the mountains and man-made structures are temporary at best. PL

ADDRESS 24955 Pacific Coast Highway, Malibu 90265 [628–H7]
CLIENT Ron Goldman
STRUCTURAL ENGINEER Murashige Onishi
SIZE 20,500 square feet (1900 square metres)
COST $1.8 million
ACCESS none

Malibu

**Goldman/Firth/Boccato Architects 1988**

Goldman/Firth/Boccato Architects 1988

**Gray Residence**

This oceanside house is defined by an exposed concrete framework of Brutalist proportions. Presenting a sombre but well-balanced face to the thunderous traffic that blasts down the Pacific Coast Highway, the 2.1.2 rhythm of its bays, combined with set-backs at ground level for motor access and a pediment over its central bay, nevertheless manage to keep it relatively light on its feet. Infilled at the higher level with the same Indian red sandstone as Isozaki used at MOCA and by a wall of glass block, the house has a restrained and aloof presence, touched with antiquity.

If its street face is forbidding, the view of the house from the shoreline is quite different. The concrete grid, now three storeys high as it steps down to the sea, is revealed as an armature for extensive glazing, and the whole building appears filled with light.

Internal spaces flow one into another and the double-height living areas and glass-block walls and floors make the spaces seem linked by light. PL

ADDRESS 20858 Pacific Coast Highway, Malibu 90265 [630–F6]
CLIENT David and Karen Gray
STRUCTURAL ENGINEER Dimitry Vergun
SIZE 3500 square feet (325 square metres)
COST $1.3 million
ACCESS none

**Malibu**

**David Lawrence Gray Architects 1990**

# Pacific Palisades and Brentwood

# Keeler Residence

This house is built on a sloping site with two access points – one from the street at the bottom of the site and the other from a driveway at the top. This double access provided the basis for the design.

A single-run stair was created to connect the two entries. This bisects the house and determines the position of the carefully hand-crafted living areas. There are open-plan living spaces in the upper levels on both sides of the stair, with bedrooms below. The stair itself is made of laminated glass, allowing light to filter down to the lowest level.

The house relates to the stunning tower-system house Ray Kappe designed for his own family in 1967. In the case of the Keeler Residence, the structure is supported by three concrete tower units which together with two front columns take the seismic and vertical loads. The exterior is characterised by thrusting decks and roof overhangs. Materials are predominantly wood, concrete and large panes of undivided glass, which make the view an integral part of the interior.

Though the formal entrance is from Akron Street, the most dramatic experience of the house is from the upper carport entrance above. Standing at the glass galleria above the descending stairway, one experiences a breathtaking view through the double-volume spaces, over the outdoor decks and out towards the ocean.

ADDRESS 16525 Akron Street, Pacific Palisades 90272 [630–H4]
CLIENT Anne Keeler
STRUCTURAL ENGINEER Reiss Brown Ekmekji
ACCESS none

**Pacific Palisades/Brentwood**

**Kappe Architects Planners 1990**

**Kappe Architects Planners 1990**

# St Matthew's Episcopal Church

When the previous church was destroyed by fire in 1978, MRY was asked to involve the parish in planning and designing its replacement. Through workshops involving architects, consultants and members of the congregation, a schematic design was created. The congregants were divided. Some wanted a traditional, lofty, symmetrical church with a minimum of glass and wood (for liturgical and acoustic reasons); other wanted a more informal and rustic building with intimately placed seating, extensive use of wood and a close relationship to the landscape. The result – in which the cruciform plan of the roof and upper walls is cut away at ground level to make space for seven rows of semicircular seating – accommodates all of this.

A traditional nave and transept rise above a large California-style hipped roof which is cut into as a response to existing trees. The ceiling is wood with open beams; walls are covered with plaster appliquéd with a system of wood battens patterned like traceries.

As can happen with Charles Moore's work, the internal space contains too much. But the building is lofty and inspiring. Skylights fill it with soft daylight, windows look outside to the trees and the prayer garden, and a small transparent chapel connects with the landscape.

The First Church of Christ Scientist at 1320 North Brand Boulevard in Glendale is also the work of Moore Ruble Yudell.

ADDRESS 1031 Bienveneda Avenue, Pacific Palisades 90272 [630–H5]
STRUCTURAL ENGINEER Kurily Szymanski Tchirkow
ACCESS open

**Moore Ruble Yudell Architects 1983**

# Lederer Residence

Because of its elaborate tile-work, the front elevation of the pre-existing 1922 Spanish-style house on the Lederer Residence site was declared an historic monument. So it was saved and displays itself to the narrow street, while Finn Kappe's concrete-block structure looms behind it, cantilevering over the East Rustic Canyon.

The house is built on a long, narrow site and the outside is repeatedly brought inside through glazed walls, skylights and the glass-roofed courtyard, which acts as a passive solar heater. The tile-work from other parts of the original house has been saved and re-used throughout Kappe's modern spaces.

The new work is best seen from Mesa Drive across the canyon, or from East Rustic below.

**Pacific Palisades/Brentwood**

ADDRESS 390 Vance Street, Pacific Palisades 90272 [631–B7]
CLIENTS Dave and Margaret Lederer
STRUCTURAL ENGINEER Dimitry Vergun
SIZE 3000 square feet (280 square metres)
ACCESS none

**Finn Kappe, Architect 1992**

**Finn Kappe, Architect 1992**

# Schwartz Residence

A steel cube frame is anchored to the ground at four points where it rests on concrete piers. Inside the frame is a rotated, solid cube structured in steel and clad with corrugated galvanised-metal sheets and large panes of clear and sandblasted glass. Slipped beneath the frame is a concrete-block box for parking, with roof decks on top. This solution has allowed the living quarters to pivot away from the heat of the west sun and to gain views down the canyon road rather than looking directly across the street. It also simplifies the foundation system, which is kept parallel to the slope of the site.

Inside, two floors of living space are connected by a bright yellow spiral staircase with open-plan living below and bedrooms above. Walls are white-painted plasterboard that stop short of the ceiling so that the structure of the box is revealed. Where necessary, sandblasted glass is used to provide privacy in this tight canyon, while clear glass allows for the canyon views.

ADDRESS 444 Sycamore Road, Santa Monica 90402 [631–B7]
CLIENT Martin Schwartz
STRUCTURAL ENGINEER Dimitry Vergun
SIZE 2700 square feet (250 square metres) and 400-square-foot (37-square-metre) garage
ACCESS none

**Pierre Koenig, Architect 1994**

**Pacific Palisades/Brentwood**

**Pierre Koenig, Architect 1994**

**Canyon House**

This house has an enviable location – a hilltop in a canyon with wide ocean views. By dividing the house into three identifiable masses – a block, a tower and a connecting mass – Cigolle + Coleman have created a stunning home for themselves which is a place for family and work, and which capitalises on all aspects of the steeply sloping site.

Despite its size, the house never reads as a monolith or a sprawl. From the street one sees only the top storey of the block, with its elegantly understated elevation which houses the architectural office and parking garage. From across the canyon the structure reads as a set of differently shaped volumes, while from the side a mix of cladding materials (plaster, wood, copper and zinc-coated tiles) breaks up the mass and creates a compelling composition.

The internal layout consists of work spaces at the top, living spaces in the middle and bedrooms at the bottom. The block contains a series of loft spaces – large and open with exposed wooden ceiling structures and views out to the canyon. The tower's rooms are square in plan with views towards the ocean. The connecting mass, defined by a straight and a curving wall, contains a terrace, dining room and master bathroom.

A good view can be had from Vance Street on the other side of the canyon.

ADDRESS 455 Upper Mesa Road, Santa Monica 90402 [631–B7]
CLIENTS Mark Cigolle and Kim Coleman
STRUCTURAL ENGINEERS Dimitry Vergun, Issak Basman
ACCESS none

**Pacific Palisades/Brentwood**

**Cigolle + Coleman 1991**

**Cigolle + Coleman 1991**

**Mesa Road House**

The only part of the Mesa Road House that faces the tight canyon road is a standard garage – an independent structure with a tunnel through the middle flanked on either side by single-car parking. From the shadows of this tunnel the house comes into view – a five-storey, elegantly symmetrical white stucco building at the far end of a ravine filled with sunlight, big eucalyptus trees, plants and flowers. Three long catwalks supported by pipe columns and cross-bracing cables radiate back towards the street at different angles and from different floors, connecting to different levels of the terraced hillside. To enter the living room you have the exhilarating experience of crossing an 80-foot-long bridge some 50 feet in the air.

The house is made up of four floors, each with the same plan of a single room with wings on either side that contain stairs and bathrooms, plus a top-floor lofted area. The ground floor is an office/bedroom, the second the master suite, the third the kitchen and dining room, and the fourth the living room. Forty-seven French doors (the maximum allowed by the building code), dozens of portholes and some skylights flood every floor with daylight.

The story goes that the owners took a vacation to Hawaii but cut it short when they realised that no other paradise equalled the one at home.

ADDRESS 509 Mesa Road, Santa Monica 90402 [631–B7]
STRUCTURAL ENGINEER Joseph A Perazzelli
SIZE 1750 square feet (163 square metres)
COST $128,000
ACCESS none

**Pacific Palisades/Brentwood**

**BAM Construction/Design Inc 1985**

**BAM Construction/Design Inc 1985**

**Cookston Residence**

The strong vertical thrust and concrete-block and glass construction make this house a departure from other canyon houses designed by Ray Kappe. But it does contain qualities consistent with his earlier work such as the open-plan, split-level living spaces and large areas of glass that connect the inside to the outside.

The house is laid out with a shop, studio and guest bedroom on the first floor, the main living spaces on the second floor and the master suite on the third. There is an uninterrupted penetration of space from the studio to the master bedroom.

The house is a passive-designed structure that uses concrete-block walls and concrete floors to increase the mass. The all-glass south face feeds the sun to an east–west wall that divides the house in two. The heated air collected from the high point of the curved south section is drawn to the rock storage-area by fan, stored during the day and then released through the back-up heating system in the evening. Solar collectors integrated into the south-facing wall provide for the hot water heating and act as a reinforcement for the passive systems incorporated in the design.

ADDRESS 762 Latimer Road, Pacific Palisades 90272 [631–C6]
CLIENTS Mr and Mrs Steve Cookston
STRUCTURAL ENGINEER Reiss Brown Ekmekji
ACCESS none

Pacific Palisades/Brentwood

**Kappe Architects Planners 1984**

**Pacific Palisades/Brentwood**

**Kappe Architects Planners 1984**

**Kappe Pool House**

At the top of the sloping property of Ray and Shelly Kappe's 1967 house is a small, level piece of land. It is high enough in the canyon to receive uninterrupted sunlight, and has been developed into their own private resort, with a sunken jacuzzi, lap pool and wedge-shaped pool house.

The pool house presents itself as a mute wall of redwood siding and forms a vertical edge to the lap pool, with a single opening where a table and chairs are placed. Otherwise, there is a linear sequence of an equipment room, sauna, kitchen, dressing area and bathroom. The equipment room and sauna are covered; all the other spaces are open to the sky beneath the canopy of a thick flowering vine.

This is a simple, serene spot.

**Pacific Palisades/Brentwood**

ADDRESS 715 Brooktree Road, Pacific Palisades 90272 [631-B6]
CLIENTS Ray and Shelly Kappe
SIZE 188 square feet (17 square metres)
ACCESS none

**Kappe Architects Planners 1984**

**Kappe Architects Planners 1984**

**Benton Residence**

Approaching this house, one is struck by the beauty of its surroundings and the exquisiteness of its structure. Nestled within the canyon, it seems to emit a glow from the concrete, large expanses of glass and the jewel-like quality of the hand-picked Douglas fir.

The house was originally designed as an addition to an existing house on the site. The main living areas are accommodated in a generous uninterrupted space at first-floor level. A large open stairway leads up to the gallery from which are accessed the bedrooms and office on the upper level, where the original house once stood. Both levels share the same ceiling, giving a soaring height to the lower space. The siting has respected the existing major trees and opens the house up to a breathtaking canyon view. The orientation is such that the Title 24 Energy Code has been met with single glazing throughout.

**Pacific Palisades/Brentwood**

ADDRESS 136 Canyon View Drive, Los Angeles 90049 [631–F4]
CLIENT Dr Esther Benton
STRUCTURAL ENGINEER Reiss Brown Ekmekji
ACCESS none

**Kappe Architects Planners 1994**

**Pacific Palisades/Brentwood**

**Kappe Architects Planners 1994**

**Koenig Residence**

Despite changes in architectural fashion, Pierre Koenig has continued to produce clean, elegant, industrial solutions for buildings using methods and an aesthetic he developed in the 1950s.

This steel and glass house is constructed in prefabricated bents 30 feet long and about 10 feet high which were shipped to the site, erected and locked into position with tie-beams and specially designed 'moment' connections that allow free use of the space and clear spans. The centre of the house is a 30-foot-high enclosed atrium which most of the living areas open on to. To mitigate its impact on the surrounding one- and two-storey buildings, the house steps back in three graduated levels before reaching its full height.

Koenig is a serious advocate of natural ventilation to cool the interior of a building. Here, cool-wind ventilation is introduced through a special 'wind' door on the first floor with exhaust exits located throughout, but especially at the third level of the atrium. Large industrial fans have been provided for days with no wind. Designed with natural forces in mind, the sun's penetration is minimised in the summer and maximised in the winter.

ADDRESS 12221 Dorothy Street, Los Angeles 90049 [631–G5]
CLIENT Pierre Koenig
STRUCTURAL ENGINEER Dimitry Vergun
SIZE 3000 square feet (280 square metres) and 600-square-foot (565-square-metre) carport
ACCESS none

**Pierre Koenig, Architect 1985**

**Pierre Koenig, Architect 1985**

# Santa Monica

**Montana Collection**

Located on a prestigious shopping street in an equally prestigious neighbourhood that is trying to keep development in check, the Montana Collection is far from the standard LA corner mall. Trying to maintain the ambience of a 'walk street' and to keep to the scale of the residential buildings around it, double-height retail spaces line Montana Avenue with parking discretely removed to the roof. The façade is broken into a number of seemingly autonomous architectural elements in an attempt to minimise its visual impact. A ribbon of stucco, punctured at intervals by small windows, gives way to a steel and glass element that in turn contrasts with the more substantial barrel-vaulted structure that anchors the corner. From this, a wavy parapet flows towards the stair and elevator tower on 14th Street.

After completion of this project, but not, apparently, as a direct result of it, rooftop parking joined subterranean parking on the prohibited list in this area in an attempt to reduce the scale of future developments. PL

ADDRESS 1406 Montana Avenue, Santa Monica 90403 [631–D7]
CLIENT Christina Development
STRUCTURAL ENGINEER Wong, Hobach & Lau Consulting Engineeers
SIZE 10,000 square feet (930 square metres)
COST $1.5 million
ACCESS open

**Kanner Architects 1989**

**Kanner Architects 1989**

# House, 25th Street

Perhaps it is not surprising, given LA's history of immigrant architects, that this house, which so strongly continues the Southern Californian tradition of linking internal and external spaces, should have been designed by two Australians.

A simple barrel-vaulted volume, two storeys high and only 17 feet wide, runs down the north side of the 50 by 167 foot plot. A large sliding door opens from the kitchen – the heart of the building – on to the garden, effectively turning the outside space into another room. Bougainvillea, grape, wisteria and trumpet vine climb the arbor that runs above this doorway, shading the house from the sun.

A 'garden pavilion', square in plan and skewed from the axis of the body of the house, stands closest to the street. The lower level living room looks out over the 'meadow', or less cultivated part of the garden, while the studio above opens on to a balcony. The dark green stucco used for this part of the building, with diamond-pattern wire trellising and heavily glazed top floor, give it a strong visual presence, while the slight twist in its placement breaks up the regularity of the composition and creates an interesting trapezoidal entryway. Broad wooden battens over a glazed wall break sunlight into horizontal bands in this area.

Rooms are refreshingly compact, but the confident use of colour, easy movement from space to space and ever-present garden views mean they never feel cramped.

The garage shows how resourceful the architects have been. Set apart from the house at the rear of the lot, it is a simple structure made special by the strips of lathe used to enclose the space. In the same way that the entrance to the house is filled with broken light, the garage is filled with shafts of sunlight streaming in between the narrow lathes.

The project's greatest strength is the integration of building and garden.

Santa Monica

**Koning Eizenberg Architecture 1989**

**Koning Eizenberg Architecture 1989**

The landscaping, which was conceived as an 'urban forest' in deference to the rich growth in neighbouring gardens, was integral to the design and only now, with the maturation of sycamores, lemon gums and eucalyptus four years after constuction was completed, is that vision coming to fruition. PL

ADDRESS 909 25th Street, Santa Monica 90403 [631–F6]
CLIENT Hank Koning and Julie Eizenberg
STRUCTURAL ENGINEER The Office of Gordon Polon
LANDSCAPE Robert Fletcher
SIZE 2700 square feet (250 square metres)
COST $380,000
ACCESS none

**Koning Eizenberg Architecture 1989**

Santa Monica

**Koning Eizenberg Architecture 1989**

# 2nd Street Townhouses

Positioned next to the parking lot for the local church, this condominium building of four three-storey units can be seen on three sides. Bedrooms are at ground level, the double-height living space, dining and kitchen areas are at the second level with a loft at the top.

In designing the elevations, William Adams was interested in expressing the 'three basic material methods of making shelters', which he identifies as 'primitive earthen materials, gathered stick materials and nomadic or preassembled materials'. These are represented by stucco, wood shingles, and zinc and steel, and are used along with the massing to articulate the individual units, to separate the functions visually and to provide contemporary ornament. There is no relying on unnecessary contrivances to make clever architecture.

William Adams has also designed a set of condominiums at 245–251 Ocean Park Boulevard, Santa Monica and four subsidised housing projects at 1544 Berkeley Street, 1747 15th Street, 1828 17th Street and 1968 19th Street.

ADDRESS 2318 2nd Street, Santa Monica 90405 [671–F4]
CLIENTS Ian and Tobby Kippen
STRUCTURAL ENGINEER Parker-Resnick
SIZE four units of 1600 square feet (150 square metres) each
ACCESS none

Santa Monica

**William Adams 1989**

**William Adams 1989**

# Broadway Deli

Strong graphics, a restrained palette of materials and colours and a lot of salami give this deli and restaurant a distinctly New York feel.

A black polished concrete floor anchors the large open space, while a ceiling of raw white plaster opens it up. Grey plaster walls and grey window frames are unobtrusive foils for the views out on to the street and into the kitchen and delicatessen. An end wall of ply squares stained a glowing orange illuminates the whole space.

Despite a sense that the dining area is perhaps a little too open, this is a deft and sophisticated reinterpretation of an American institution. PL

Santa Monica

ADDRESS 1457 3rd Street Promenade, Santa Monica 90401 [671–D1]
CLIENTS Bruce Marder, Michel Richard, Marvin Zeidler
SIZE 10,000 square feet (930 square metres)
COST $2 million
ACCESS open

**Steven Ehrlich Architects 1990**

**Steven Ehrlich Architects 1990**

**Fama**

Over-scaled, maple-veneered plywood structures give this small restaurant its character. The centrepiece is an abstract primitive hut which accommodates the hostess area and has a sloping floor that connects the two levels. Abstract structures that recall tree trunks cover existing columns and beams. A rear wall enclosing additional seating on an upper level is treated like an exterior wall. Large storefront windows on to a busy pavement add to the illusion of being on the terrace of a sidewalk café.

Rockenwagner at 2345 Main Street, Santa Monica, is another restaurant designed by David Kellen as an abstraction of an outdoor space.

ADDRESS 1416 4th Street, Santa Monica 90401 [671–E3]
CLIENTS Hans and Mary Rockenwagner
STRUCTURAL ENGINEER Les Fejes
SIZE 1800 square feet (170 square metres)
COST $135,000
ACCESS restaurant hours

**David Kellen 1989**

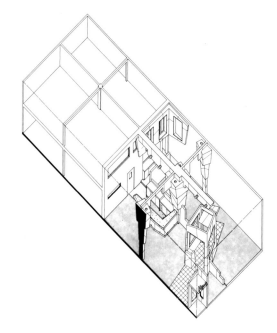

**Santa Monica**

**David Kellen 1989**

**Border Grill**

The walls and ceiling of a black box are decorated with exuberant murals by Sue Huntley and Donna Muir. A large-scale, irregularly shaped, pumpkin-coloured fence divides the room in two, with the bar on one side and the dining area on the other. The furniture designed by Josh Schweitzer introduces a more human scale.

This loud and boisterous restaurant is a fine setting for some of LA's best Mexican food.

Santa Monica

ADDRESS 1445 4th Street, Santa Monica 90401 [671–E2]
CLIENTS Mary Sue Milliken and Susan Feniger
SIZE 4500 square feet (420 square metres)
ACCESS restaurant hours

**Schweitzer BIM 1989**

**Santa Monica**

**Schweitzer BIM 1989**

# Ken Edwards Center

The Ken Edwards Center takes a complex programme and renders it in an humane fashion. The building houses two independent agencies that provide health and counselling services and a lunch programme for Santa Monica's elderly. It also acts as a community conference centre.

Wanting to avoid both institutional blandness and patronising kitsch, the architects have rendered the front elevation as three discrete elements: a simple box with a hipped roof, a flat-roofed box set back from the street and skewed away from the orthogonal, and a seemingly disconnected barrel-vaulted structure, elevated above the passenger drop-off. A set of stairs leads directly from the street up to a central courtyard located at second-floor level.

Although evidently well liked by the people who use the facilities, two aspects of the design seem less than successful: the passenger drop-off is unappealing and the courtyard is barren. PL

ADDRESS 1527 4th Street, Santa Monica 90401 [671–F3]
CLIENT City of Santa Monica
STRUCTURAL ENGINEER Freet, Yeh, Rosenbach
SIZE 25,000 square feet (2300 square metres), including two-and-a-half levels of underground parking
COST $4.2 million
ACCESS none

**Koning Eizenberg Architecture 1990**

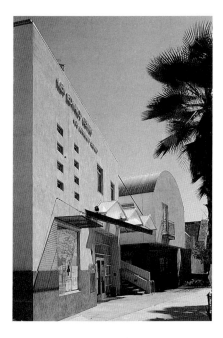

**Santa Monica**

**Koning Eizenberg Architecture 1990**

# Bikini

An exuberant splash of texture, elegance and colour, this space sits in a two-storey shopfront four blocks from the beach. Display of the patrons and references to the ocean are the order of the day.

The articulation of the double-volume eating area, mezzanine gallery, bar and entrance is supported by the ceiling design in which materials, forms and colours change in accordance with the spaces they cover to create a richly varied composition.

The beach references are consistent throughout but not too obvious. At the entrance stands a waterfall designed by Eric Orr. The far wall in the main dining area is a rich cherry-dyed plywood curve dubbed 'the wave'. Terrazzo recalls the sand and pebbles of the beach and the booths upstairs are boldly coloured and eccentrically curved to suggest bandeau tops. Muramasa Kudo painted the mural depicting sea nymphs.

Santa Monica

ADDRESS 1413 5th Street, Santa Monica 90401 [631–E2]
CLIENT John Sedlar
STRUCTURAL ENGINEER Helfman/Haloossim
SIZE 3500 square feet (325 square metres), including outside patio
ACCESS open

**Brantner Design Associates 1991**

Santa Monica

**Brantner Design Associates 1991**

# Offices, 7th Street

A simple and elegant grid of poured-in-place concrete forms a *brise soleil* for this taut, muscular structure. Reminiscent of Le Corbusier's Carpenter Center at Harvard, it is a statement of confidence in the ideals of Modernism in contrast to the thinly applied façades around it. Two bays wide by four high, it fronts a long, narrow office building topped by a curved roof of translucent Kalwall. A brightly painted earthquake-bracing framework of exposed steel overlays the grid like the ghostly remains of some other structure.

The concrete structural skeleton is infilled with Schindleresque glazing panels which look out at the side on to elevator towers and exposed gantry-like walkways, as well as on to a courtyard garden that pays homage to the Italian architect Carlo Scarpa. A feeling of closeness to the elements – the sound of a fountain in the garden, the glow of sunlight through the Kalwall, the breezes one feels on the walkways – places this building firmly in the Southern Californian tradition of uniting architecture and nature. Full of latent energy, it seems to sit implacably waiting for everything around it to fall down. PL

Santa Monica

ADDRESS 1546 7th Street, Santa Monica 90401 [671–D1]
CLIENT 7th Street Limited
STRUCTURAL ENGINEER Dimitry Vergun
SIZE 25,000 square feet (2300 square metres)
COST $2.6 million
ACCESS by appointment

**David Lawrence Gray Architects 1991**

Clearance 7'-0"

Santa Monica

**David Lawrence Gray Architects 1991**

**Edgemar Development**

Abby Sher's enthusiasm for bringing a museum to Main Street, Santa Monica was sparked when artist Tom Eatherton suggested using the site that had once been the Edgemar Dairy. He had earlier approached some of the Los Angeles museums with the idea, but they were not interested in establishing a satellite here. The idea took hold and Sher became the founder of the Santa Monica Museum, the centrepiece of this development.

In order to maintain the scale of the shops that line Main Street, the 250-foot-wide frontage has been filled with five small, visually separate structures. The central element is a rebuilt wall fragment of the former dairy, clad in seafoam-green tile and copper. Two narrow passageways on either side of this piece take you into the central courtyard which is lined with shops, a restaurant and the Santa Monica Museum (interior by Lubowicki Lanier) at ground level with offices above. In keeping with the spirit of the shopping centre as a cultivated place, some of the retail space is taken by a bookstore, a photographic gallery and the Gallery of Functional Art.

Three transparent towers – one an open steel frame, one a greenhouse structure and the third draped in signature chain-link fence – remind one of San Gimignano, maybe due to its proximity to Venice…

ADDRESS 2435 Main Street, Santa Monica 90405 [671–E3]
CLIENT Sher Development/Santa Monica Museum of Art
STRUCTURAL ENGINEER Kurily Szymanski Tchirkow
SIZE 34,500 square feet (3200 square metres) with parking for 103 cars
COST $3 million
ACCESS open

**Santa Monica**

**Frank O Gehry and Associates 1988**

**Santa Monica**

**Frank O Gehry and Associates 1988**

**Harriet Dorn**

O'Herlihy + Warner's second interior design for the Harriet Dorn clothing store in the Edgemar complex (the first was for customised display units placed around the perimeter) fully exploits the proportions and qualities of the space. Filling Frank Gehry's skylit tower is a mobile-like steel assemblage which makes the entire volume into a hanging display for women's garments. Faceted maple cupboards create a backdrop and a linen canopy diffuses the sunlight.

**Santa Monica**

ADDRESS 2423 Main Street, Santa Monica 90405 [671–F4]
CLIENT Sandra Mathers
SIZE 300 square feet (28 square metres)
COST $8000
ACCESS open

**O'Herlihy + Warner Architects 1993**

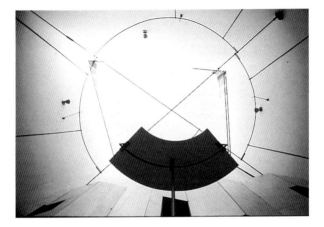

**O'Herlihy + Warner Architects 1993**

**Eli Broad Family Foundation**

The purpose of the Eli Broad Family Foundation is to build a collection of contemporary art. As part of this project, the Foundation has chosen to acquire large works that might rarely be displayed in other galleries simply because of their size. There is no problem about showing them here, however. The Foundation's galleries and offices are located in what used to be a telephone-switching station, and the internal spaces of the four-storey, 1927 building have been stripped back to industrial-sized emptiness. Ceilings up to 16 feet in height allow even the largest Julian Schnabel mixed-media to be hung in the dazzlingly white, loft-like galleries.

Restraint and revelation are the watchwords of this project, but where the architects have made interventions, they are telling. The top three floors have been fitted with huge French doors to facilitate the movement of large canvases in and out of the building. The doors are left exposed, and help fill the galleries with sunlight. In the entry lobby, black terrazzo, verde jade marble and blood wood create an atmosphere reminiscent of an Art Deco apartment block.

The exterior has been left largely untouched, but the blocking of the ground-floor arcade with walls of concrete makes for an alienating street-scape. PL

ADDRESS 3355 Barnard Way, Santa Monica 90405 [671–F4]
CLIENT Eli Broad Family Foundation
STRUCTURAL ENGINEER John A Martin & Associates
SIZE 25,000 square feet (2300 square metres)
COST $1.25 million
ACCESS by appointment

Santa Monica

**Frederick Fisher, Architect 1988**

**Frederick Fisher, Architect 1988**

**Sony Music Campus**

This project for Sony Music Entertainment is a courtyard design that accommodates the Sony, Columbia and Epic companies in three separate buildings. The entrances and a restaurant face the interior courtyard, which is filled with water fountains and bamboo in an attempt to create an oasis in this light industrial area.

The lobbies to Sony and Epic are quietly elegant. The Columbia lobby, with its double-volume height, exposed ceiling structure, skylighting, galleries and staircase, is more dramatic.

The painted-stucco courtyard elevations are rather nondescript, but careful attention has been given to the street elevations. Clad in red sandstone, clear glass and green opaque glass, these make reference to streamline Moderne architecture and to musical notation. The corner has been strongly acknowledged by the tight circular curve of one building abutting the acutely angled corner of another.

With all the gesturing of these public elevations, one expects to find a street entrance, but this is at the far end of the Colorado Avenue façade. A ramp down to subterranean parking is encircled by a driveway scaled to accommodate the stretch limousines that drop off guests and celebrities, who then pass through sculpted metal gates (by Guy Dill) and progress through the courtyard to the buildings.

ADDRESS 2100 Colorado Avenue, Santa Monica 90404 [631–G7]
CLIENT Santa Monica Place Partners
STRUCTURAL ENGINEER Ismail & Otova
INTERIOR DESIGNER Cosimo Pizzulli
SIZE 100,000 square feet (9300 square metres)
COST $15 million
ACCESS by appointment; telephone (310) 449 2100

Santa Monica

**Steven Ehrlich Architects 1992**

Santa Monica

**Steven Ehrlich Architects 1992**

**Opus**

An isolated roadside steel and canvas kiosk announces the presence of this restaurant in the monstrous Water Garden Business Park. Having left the car with the valet, the customer walks along a serpentine path that leads to a corner entrance.

Inside, Jeffrey Daniels has created a more elegant version of his earlier restaurant, Typhoon (see page 84). There is an extensive use of wood throughout, this time pearwood, and the focus is directed through a glazed wall to the spectacle outside – in this case the romantic waterscape at the centre of the business park. Inside, a number of curving elements add to the sensuous atmosphere. The intimacy of the rooms, the warm use of materials and the excellent acoustics make for a delicious, if exclusive, environment.

Santa Monica

ADDRESS 2425 Olympic Boulevard, Santa Monica 90404 [631–H7]
CLIENTS Charles Almond and Eberhard Mueller
STRUCTURAL ENGINEER Robert Englekirk Consulting Engineers, Inc
SIZE 4800 square feet (450 square metres)
ACCESS restaurant hours

**Grinstein/Daniels 1992**

**Grinstein/Daniels 1992**

# The Peter Boxenbaum Arts Education Center

The Crossroads School is made up of a row of converted warehouses that front 21st Street and frame a private alley that functions as a social centre and parking lot. MRY were asked to convert another warehouse into a new facility for visual and performing arts.

The programme required studios for dance, art and music along with classrooms, an exhibition gallery and a performance space. The elevation is simple and expressive of the plan. The core of the building is an internal street that leads to a double-height atrium – an articulation of the school's missing quadrangle. Light monitors along the roof fill this postmodern space with daylight and a grand stairway and upper-level gallery lend a strong presence.

**Santa Monica**

ADDRESS 1714 21st Street, Santa Monica 90404 [671 –G1]
CLIENT Crossroads School
STRUCTURAL ENGINEER Robert Englekirk Consulting Engineers, Inc
SIZE 15,000 square feet (1400 square metres)
COST $2.3 million
ACCESS by appointment; telephone (310) 829 7391

**Moore Ruble Yudell Architects 1989**

Santa Monica

**Moore Ruble Yudell Architects 1989**

# 2200 Michigan Avenue

This fortress stands in a rapidly changing light-industrial area and overlooks the Santa Monica Freeway. It is clad with a custom-made, vertically split faced concrete block giving texture to walls that are otherwise free of ornament or detail. Car parking occupies the ground-floor level, with office space above. On the second floor, two independent volumes, one single-storey and the other two storeys high, face each other across an open courtyard.

2200 Michigan Avenue was constructed during a building moratorium, and only 10,000 square feet of office space were allowed. To increase this, plans were submitted for a element resembling a child's climbing structure that would be slotted independently into the double-volume space. An additional 3500 square feet of upper-level work stations were obtained when the structure was permitted as a functional sculpture.

Internally, the building is left as a basic shell, exposing all structural materials. The ceiling is a clutter of open-web trusses, conduits, ducts and suspended lighting. The overwhelming feature is the 'Jungle Gym' fabricated from bright red circular steel sections that define the upper- and lower-level work stations and provide second-storey circulation.

ADDRESS 2200 Michigan Avenue, Santa Monica 90404 [671 –F2]
CLIENT Ralph E Phillips Consulting Engineers and Pacific Architects Collaborative
STRUCTURAL ENGINEER Martin & Huang
SIZE 13,500 square feet (1250 square metres)
ACCESS none

Santa Monica

**Arthur Pereira, AIA 1983**

Santa Monica

**Arthur Pereira, AIA 1983**

# DC-3

This restaurant sits on the third floor of the Supermarine Complex at Santa Monica Airport and spans the 100-foot-wide aircraft display court-yard of the adjacent Museum of Flying. To reach the restaurant you ride a steel and glass elevator which stands independent of the main building, cross into the building on an open-air catwalk and finally enter a black fossilised-granite cube to meet the hostess.

The huge volume has been broken down through the use of a series of sculptural objects. A freestanding black plaster sphere houses the entry cube. A 40-foot-wide, floor-to-ceiling wood and glass grid wall separates the bar from the main dining area. A rusted-steel 'Lunch Pail' houses the liquor at the vast cowhide-clad bar. And a geometric, smooth plaster-finished freeform contains the restrooms.

The materials used range from steel, aluminium and glass to natural stones, woods and animal hides.

Santa Monica

ADDRESS 2800 Donald Douglas Loop North, Santa Monica 90405 [672–A2]
CLIENT Bruce Marder
STRUCTURAL ENGINEER Brian Cochran and Associates
ACCESS open

**Solberg + Lowe with Chuck Arnoldi 1988**

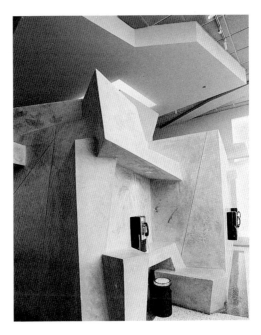

Santa Monica

**Solberg + Lowe with Chuck Arnoldi 1988**

# Typhoon

Jeffrey Daniels has designed a stylish and unpretentious room located in the administration building at Santa Monica Airport. It sits within glazed walls one level above the airfield and fully exploits the spectacle of the airport's activity There was little opportunity for design of the front elevation, but the back elevation curves exuberantly on to the airfield and looks like a flattened control tower.

There is an unmistakeable air of romance inside. An extensive use of wood – cherry in this case – seems to emphasise the 'nautical' in aeronautical. A mirrored weather map of the world hangs over the bar and metal lamps carved with symbols for weather systems are suspended above the booths.

Late afternoon is the best time to sip a drink and watch commuter traffic taking off to the west, flying over the ocean and disappearing towards the horizon.

**Santa Monica**

ADDRESS 3221 Donald Douglas Loop, Santa Monica 90405 [672–A2]
CLIENT Brian Vidor
STRUCTURAL ENGINEER Richard C C Lee
SIZE 5000 square feet (465 square metres)
COST $700,000
ACCESS open

**Grinstein/Daniels 1991**

**Grinstein/Daniels 1991**

# Venice

**Ocean Front Walk Condominiums**

These stunning condominiums rest on the edge of the beach like a fish out of water. To the north is the architecturally undistinguished Sea Colony, and to the south the pleasant tackiness of the Venice Boardwalk. The Ocean Front Walk block, with its good proportions, concrete-coloured plaster and black-painted steel frames, appears to have arrived in its Armani suit instead of its bathing suit.

The building consists of five independent structures that house two units apiece and have an A-B-B-B-C rhythm. The expressed-steel 'moment' frames satisfy seismic regulations and allow for entirely glazed fronts with breathtaking ocean views.

These condominiums show that one doesn't have to dress down to come to the beach: a more urban vision is appropriate too.

ADDRESS 101–119 Ocean Front Walk, Venice 90291 [671–F5]
CLIENT Ocean Front Walk Townhomes Partnership
STRUCTURAL ENGINEER The Office of Gordon Polon
SIZE 33,000 square feet (3000 square metres)
ACCESS none

**Venice**

**L Anthony Greenberg AIA 1993**

**L Anthony Greenberg AIA 1993**

**Bleifer Residence**

The programme for this house is as interesting as the architecture. It is designed for an artist and a wine connoisseur who is also an avid fisherman.

Two pavilions sit on a plinth. The front block houses the main living quarters and the back block holds the artist's studio with guest accommodation. The pavilions are connected at ground level via an enclosed terrace and at gallery level via a glass bridge.

As in many of Frederick Fisher's houses, the primary space – accommodating the living room, dining room and kitchen – is designed like a New York loft, the entire floor being one large open space with high ceilings that expose the structure. The floor above consists of a spacious master-bedroom suite and the basement contains a wine cellar which can hold 4000 bottles, a wine-tasting room which opens on to a rock garden and a third room that offers storage and organisation for the client's equally vast collection of fishing gear. The roof terrace has sweeping ocean views.

Across the courtyard is the double-height studio where Sandra Bleifer creates her paper sculptures. There is a small office space at gallery level to the studio with guest accommodation and two small studies above.

This house is sited on a busy Venice walk street with heavy beach traffic. Despite this, it maintains a great sense of privacy and calm.

ADDRESS 22 Sunset Avenue, Venice 90291 [671–G5]
CLIENTS Dr Kenneth Bleifer and Sandra Bleifer
STRUCTURAL ENGINEER Parker-Resnick
SIZE 5000 square feet (465 square metres)
ACCESS none

**Venice**

**Frederick Fisher, Architect 1992**

**Venice**

**Frederick Fisher, Architect 1992**

# 72 Market Street

This restaurant is located in a building that is part of the original colonnaded area of Venice. Upon entering, one climbs a ramp into the restaurant space which is divided into two main areas – the bar (with oyster bar) and the classically simple dining room.

An ordering device of three parallel planes of glass has been set up – one at the front elevation, one dividing the bar from the dining room and one on the back wall of the dining room. The straightforward axiality of this arrangement is undermined by a room within a room that rotates off the basic geometry. To satisfy the seismic requirements for the renovation, the architects have created a centrepiece in this room. It is a highly finessed, squat, hollow column (etched by Robert Graham) that supports a tension ring that ties the exterior walls together. It stands in line with one of the columns of the front elevation and contrasts with its slender form.

Concrete, glass, slate, copper, steel and wood are used elegantly throughout.

ADDRESS 72 Market Street, Venice 90291 [671–G6]
CLIENT Tony Bill and Dudley Moore
STRUCTURAL ENGINEER The Office of Gordon Polon
SIZE 5800 square feet (540 square metres)
ACCESS open

**Morphosis 1985**

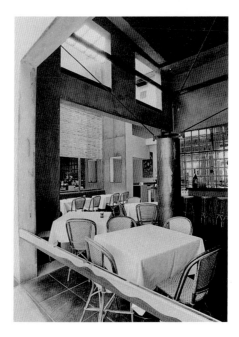

**Venice**

**Morphosis 1985**

**Rebecca's**

Upon arrival at the brick corner building that houses Rebecca's, there is no warning of the sub-aqua environment within. Reversing the evolutionary process, one arrives as a land animal and is transformed into a sea animal.

Inside, a thick glass partition separates the entry from the bar. Watching people through this is like watching fish in an aquarium. This underwater theme continues throughout. The dining area has large sculpted fish lamps, an octopus chandelier and seafoam-green padding covering the booths and walls. In the bar, crocodiles hang overhead and there are onyx-clad enclosures lit from within to create the effect of light breaking through the surface of water.

With artworks by Ed Moses, Tony Berlant and Peter Alexander, this is a lively underwater event.

ADDRESS 2025 Pacific Avenue, Venice 90291 [671–H6]
CLIENT Bruce Marder
SIZE 4450 square feet (410 square metres)
COST $1.5 million
ACCESS restaurant hours

Venice

**Frank O Gehry and Associates 1985**

**Venice**

**Frank O Gehry and Associates 1985**

# Windward Circle

Three buildings scattered around a traffic circle in what used to be the heart of Venice, Windward Circle is not the integrated development one might imagine, or hope for. Two companies were involved in developing the three sites. In a location that cries out for a vision that extends beyond the perimeter of each plot, they – or the city authorities – have been found wanting.

Full of good ideas that work better in the abstract, these structures only engage with their context at the most superficial level and add little of substance to the urban setting. Stage-set thin and already starting to age, they might yet be rescued if only someone would build a Tower of Pisa, say, on that blighted circle, or line it and the converging streets with palm trees (as the architect has suggested) – in other words, if the development was informed by planning.

Race Through the Clouds
Named for the roller coaster that previously occupied the site, this building (pictured opposite) consists of various elements pulled together by an undulating track of galvanised steel and neon that snakes around and through them. A square façade, with a hugely over-scaled window set far back into it and elevated off the ground by culvert-pipe columns, appears to float next to a cylindrical volume. Between these two stucco forms is an open stairway shielded by an industrial assemblage of wire screens.

Arts Building
Topped by structures that with the addition of a few colourful stripes

**Steven Ehrlich Architects 1989**

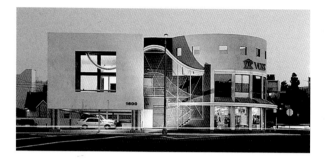

**Steven Ehrlich Architects 1989**

could be Seaside-esque bathing pavilions, this three-storey, grey plaster-faced redoubt inverts usual proportions so that from the tall top floor we descend to a squat ground floor lined with concrete-filled culvert-pipe columns and infilled with glass-block walls and rusted-steel doors. Although the ground floor has from time to time been used as retail space, this is a building that distances itself from the street.

Originally designed as artists' studios but later converted to a single-family residence, the structure completely fills its lot.

Ace Market Place
With its thin stucco façades, over-sized windows, playful distortions of scale and large Constructivist elements meant to evoke the giant steam shovels that dug Venice's original canals, this mix of shops and offices presents a sunny view of Venice. PL

ADDRESS Windward Circle, Venice 90291 [671–G6]
CLIENTS Race Through the Clouds: Voss Investments; Arts Building and Ace Market Place: Perloff & Webster
STRUCTURAL ENGINEERS Arts Building: Joseph A Perazzelli; Ace Market Place: Gary Karinen
SIZE Race Through the Clouds: 8000 square feet (740 square metres); Arts Building: 5000 square feet (460 square metres); Ace Market Place: 12,000 square feet (1100 square metres)
ACCESS Race Through the Clouds and Ace Market Place are open

**Steven Ehrlich Architects 1989**

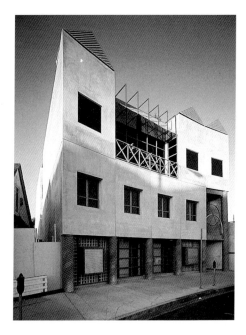

Venice

**Steven Ehrlich Architects 1989**

**Norton Residence**

This house sits on a narrow lot right on the Venice Boardwalk, and the elements presented to this busy path make for a giddy composition. Behind a concrete-block wall is an aquamarine tile-clad box framed by a driftwood arch beneath a raised 'lifeguard station'. The house is for an artist and a writer who had once been a lifeguard, and it is their workspaces that occupy these volumes.

In order to preserve privacy and maintain the ocean view, the living areas and bedrooms are raised above street level and set back at the far end of a deep terrace. The exuberance of the forms, stairs, materials and the exposed red chimney on the south wall is a response to the chaos of Venice itself.

ADDRESS 2509 Ocean Front Walk, Venice 90291 [671–G6]
CLIENTS Lynn and William Norton
STRUCTURAL ENGINEER Kurily Szymanski Tchirkow
COST $150,000
ACCESS none

Venice

**Frank O Gehry and Associates 1984**

Venice

**Frank O Gehry and Associates 1984**

# Venice Renaissance

This is indeed a rare thing for Los Angeles – a mixed-use development with a true urban section of retail on the ground floor and a mix of market-rate condominiums and low-cost rental units for senior citizens on the three floors above. Main Street is a busy retail thoroughfare and these four storeys offer a more appropriate scale to the street than the prevailing single- and two-storey structures.

The building is characterised by its references to Abbot Kinney's Venice of 1911. Arcades like those on Windward Avenue have been built at ground level and the capitals from the original columns reproduced. But the most striking (and controversial) element must be the 30-foot sculpture 'Ballerina Clown' by Jonathan Borofsky that hangs from the Rose Avenue corner.

Planning codes discourage buildings that provide a combination of commercial and residential spaces, but through the process of getting this built, a basis for a proposed City of Los Angeles ordinance on mixed-use development has been formed.

For another mixed-use development, see the architects' Janss Court at the north-east corner of Broadway and 3rd Street in Santa Monica.

ADDRESS 110 Navy Avenue, Venice 90291 [671–F4]
CLIENT Harlan Lee & Associates
STRUCTURAL ENGINEER Jitu Mehta Associates
SIZE 132,000 square feet (12,260 square metres)
COST $15 million
ACCESS ground floor only

**Venice**

**Johannes Van Tilburg & Partners 1989**

**Johannes Van Tilburg & Partners 1989**

**Chiat Day Mojo**

Located on Main Street in Venice, this building is a sign of the continued gentrification of that area. It is a three-storey structure that sits on top of three levels of underground parking. Developed initially by Frank Gehry and Greg Walsh, Chiat Day Mojo Advertising was taken on as the third partner and client, and the building was designed specifically to meet their needs.

The principal elevation has been divided into three distinctive elements. To the left is a curved screen wall which is boat-like in shape and clad in white enamelled panels. To the right is a copper-clad building with a forest of columns that take on the forms of abstracted trees. The central and primary feature is a giant pair of binoculars that stands the full height of the building and serves as a triumphal arch for the entrance of cars – after all, this is Los Angeles. It is the pedestrian who slips in at the side. This form was designed in collaboration with Claes Oldenberg and Coosje van Bruggen and was originally meant for a theatre library in Venice, Italy.

Inside, the main workspace is open plan with the individual workstations designed in ply construction to the characteristically crude precision of the Gehry office. Light is brought down to the lower floors via lightwells that occur throughout the building. There are three conference rooms with tables individually designed by Gehry. The most dramatic is the double-volume main client conference room which is on the second floor and is tied in plan to the binoculars (at this level these contain rooms with a sun oculus at the top). There is an enormous Gehry-designed light feature located centrally above the Gehry-designed table and chairs.

This is an exciting building that reflects the activity of a dynamic advertising firm. However, there is a curious sequence of spaces for visitors and clients. The first event is arrival through the binoculars. The next thing

**Frank O Gehry and Associates 1991**

**Venice**

**Frank O Gehry and Associates 1991**

one experiences is the security desk at ground level – a whimsically stunning construction of massive driftwood which fills the space and tenuously supports telephones and surveillance equipment. But the third space one encounters seems out of step   a reception area covered with Gehry-designed wallpaper *à la* Laura Ashley that creates the atmosphere of a New England inn.

ADDRESS 340 South Main Street, Venice 90291 [671–E3]
CLIENT Chiat Day Mojo Advertising
STRUCTURAL ENGINEER Wong Hobach & Lau Consulting Engineers
ASSOCIATE ARCHITECT Leidenfrost/Horowitz & Associates
SIZE 75,000 square feet (7000 square metres) plus 300-car garage
COST $15 million  (exclusive of interiors/inclusive of parking garage)
ACCESS security lobby only

**Venice**

**Frank O Gehry and Associates 1991**

**Frank O Gehry and Associates 1991**

**Venice Studios**

In the mid 1980s, Brian Murphy was asked to complete the unfinished interiors of a 1200-square-foot condominium designed by Frank Gehry. When the client decided that he needed more space he bought the lot next door and commissioned BAM to design a new house that would connect with the condominium. Behind a white picket fence and under a sweeping curved roof, this metal-clad house stands on the fringe of a section of Venice known locally as the Ghetto. As a response to this, the house treats itself like a fortress and focuses inwards.

And what a lot there is to focus on. Three linear spaces on the ground floor contain a courtyard that was originally open to the sky, a painting studio and a theatre that seats at least 40 people and is complete with stage, fly-loft, green room, dressing room, and provision for film and television production. These spaces are connected by roll-up garage doors that are arranged in a line so that large canvases can be moved throughout and trucks can deliver theatrical equipment. Living and sleeping areas are lofted upstairs.

In 1992, an addition over the courtyard provided a children's wing. This created an extraordinary space beneath a shattered-glass skylight – a garage-art gallery-kitchenette-garden (by way of a lone banana palm). The house has very few windows, as requested by the client who wanted every possible square inch of wall space to be made available for exhibiting his extensive art collection.

On entering the upper level your attention is drawn towards a ceiling supported by open-web truss joists that swells like a huge ocean wave. (Note: this curve is made entirely of straight parts.) The curves lead the eye over the low partition walls and through the various spaces – a bedroom, an open bathroom, a kitchen and a living room. Pipes and conduits hang from the underside of the ceiling and light falls through

**BAM Construction/Design Inc 1990**

**BAM Construction/Design Inc 1990**

several skylights.

Up here one sees Brian Murphy's wizardry with details. Glass is the theme. There is a large window behind the fireplace (providing a rare view to the outside) made in shattered tempered glass. The hearth around the fireplace is a tray containing crumbled tempered glass. A lamp over the dining table is a suspended, circular piece of glass again covered with crumbled glass. But the *pièce de résistance* is the freestanding sandblasted-glass bathtub. Exposed water- and jacuzzi-pipes hang off its sides and it is fluorescent-lit from below.

ADDRESS 330 Indiana Avenue, Venice 90291 [671–H5]
STRUCTURAL ENGINEER Joseph A Perazzelli
SIZE 4500 square feet (420 square metres)
COST approximately $380,000
ACCESS none

**BAM Construction/Design Inc 1990**

**BAM Construction/Design Inc 1990**

**Ward Residence**

In a rough area of Venice, Charles Ward has created a refuge for himself and for his family. The street is presented with a mute wall with two doors – one for people and one for cars. Once the wall is penetrated, one enters a place of calm and serenity. The house is a simple two-storey box with a continuous colonnade running the entire length. It is pushed to one edge of the site and a lushly planted linear courtyard with a lap pool and waterfall is created in what remains.

This is a simple, elegant and rational gesture more commonly seen in Europe. The plan is a set of linear rooms which interconnect and are linked to the courtyard by large double French doors. Materials are elemental.

The architecture shades itself from the Los Angeles movement as the colonnade shades the spaces from the Southern California glare.

ADDRESS 714 6th Avenue, Venice 90291 [671–H5]
CLIENT Charles and Ramey Ward
STRUCTURAL ENGINEER Nader Engineering
SIZE 3000 square feet (280 square metres)
ACCESS none

Venice

**Charles Ward & Associates 1988**

**Bright and Associates**

At one time the offices of Charles and Ray Eames, this building is made up of two main structures: a two-storey block and a long, pitched-roofed shed. Entry is via the block, where a light chute in the form of a parallelogram is punched through the flat roof, filling the space with natural light. A forbidding tunnel lined with sheet metal leads to the airy spaces of the shed. Here it is as if Israel is re-running the ideas he developed at Propaganda Films (see page 232) in slow motion.

Although following the same format of discrete objects built within an existing shell, the feeling is calmer and less frenetic. The space is occupied by a conference room in the form of a plywood ellipse; sensuously curved, it appears solid, finished, stable. Looking down the length of the shed, a series of regularly spaced arches reinforces the feeling of calm. The space then opens out into a large work area embraced by two curved, red stucco walls. This axis terminates in a brightly painted wall.

The exterior has been funked up in a way that adds only a confusing presence to the street and hints at the mannerism that endangers the vitality of Israel's work. PL

ADDRESS 901 Abbot Kinney Boulevard, Venice 90291 [671–G5]
CLIENT Bright and Associates
STRUCTURAL ENGINEER Davis/Fejes
SIZE 18,000 square feet (1700 square metres)
ACCESS none

Venice

**Franklin D Israel Design Associates Inc 1991**

**Franklin D Israel Design Associates Inc 1991**

**Electric ArtBlock**

Take a plot of land 50 feet wide by 360 feet long that a streetcar used to run down, an adventurous developer, imaginative architects and a helpful city ordinance. Mix them all together in Venice, and you have the ArtBlock on Electric Avenue.

Artists, long the stormtroopers of gentrification, were starting to find Venice rents less than conducive to their continued residence in the area as the influx of middle-class professionals sent land prices soaring. Conceived as a new housing prototype – the 'artist-in-residence, multi-family housing type', or, more simply put, newly built artists' lofts – the ArtBlock was made possible by a recently passed city ordinance that allowed mixed use in designated areas.

The block runs 330 feet and rises three floors over garage parking that could not be sunk completely below grade due to the high water table. It contains 20 units that range in size from 400 square feet to 1500 square feet and are either one or two storeys high. Concrete block and poured-in-place concrete form the foundation deck, above which is wooden framing clad in smooth-trowelled stucco or sheet metal. Balconies and exposed stairways are defined by chain-link fencing.

If this sounds like a megalithic intruder into the fabric of Venice, that is only half right. From Abbott Kinney Boulevard, which parallels Electric Avenue, its size is entirely appropriate. From Electric Avenue, although it dwarfs the suburban lots that face it, its assurance, swagger and avoidance of the industrial-ethos clichés that diminish so many buildings in Venice command respect.

Although the ArtBlock's presence could – and should – be humanised by the addition of a line of palm trees, the potentially soul-destroying long façade on Electric Avenue remains lively and interesting. With a wink to the streetcars that used to be seen here, it is divided into five white blocks

**Koning Eizenberg Architecture 1991**

**Koning Eizenberg Architecture 1991**

– four of which are about 40 feet wide, the fifth smaller – alternating with narrower, metal-clad and angled recesses. The feeling of movement and restlessness this creates is accentuated by the flying arches cut into the garage walls, the two-storey recesses, each painted a different colour, set into the white blocks, and the angled steel posts set within these recesses.

The studio spaces are appropriately loft-like, and at a construction cost of $36 a square foot (including the garage parking), remarkably cheap. PL

ADDRESS 499 Santa Clara, Venice 90291 [671–H5]
CLIENT Venice Art Block, Limited
ASSOCIATE ARCHITECT Glenn Robert Erikson
STRUCTURAL ENGINEER Jilla Almozafar
LANDSCAPE ARCHITECT Jay Griffith
SIZE 23,467 square feet (2180 square metres)
COST $1.62 million
ACCESS none

**Venice**

**Koning Eizenberg Architecture 1991**

**Koning Eizenberg Architecture 1991**

# Marina del Rey

**Marina Fine Arts**

For gallery-owner June Perez it was a dream come true. She had narrowed her list of architect-heroes down to five. Four of them were dead, and when asked, John Lautner agreed to take the job.

The gallery is located in a conventional shopping centre – a street-level parking lot with its far edge lined by single-storey shops. In an effort to stop people in their tracks as they pass, the entrance was designed as a freestanding metal sculpture made of two curved steel plates brightly painted in an automotive finish to look like a tulip blossom. (It is also transportable and can move with Perez if she changes locations.)

Low-tech ingenuity has been used throughout. To avoid conventional track lighting and to provide the desired daylight, skylights were built into the perimeter of the ceiling. Lights are mounted on the roof above the skylights so that the effect of daylight can be simulated at night.

The gallery faces the ocean, and steps were taken to exploit the sea breeze rather than rely on an air-conditioning system to reduce the heat generated by the lights. Decorative louvres were installed on both sides of the front to allow a flow of fresh air. Skylights that can open in the back of the space provide cross-ventilation.

Display cases, furniture and reception desk are all designed by Lautner.

**Marina del Rey**

ADDRESS 4716 Admiralty Way, Marina del Rey 90292 [672–A6]
CLIENT June Perez
SIZE 1200 square feet (110 square metres)
COST $105,000
ACCESS Monday to Friday, 10.30–18.30; Saturday 10.00–18.00; Sunday 12.00–17.00

**John Lautner Architect 1991**

**John Lautner Architect 1991**

**Levine II Residence**

The second of three houses designed for Fredric Levine by the office of Frederick Fisher, Architect, the programme was to accommodate a man and his two sons on a small site (35 feet wide by 83 feet long) on one of the walk streets in the Marina del Rey.

The client wanted the house to have a sense of open space and natural light. The challenge of bringing light into the central area was met by creating a 38-foot-tall atrium on to which the kitchen and living room open at ground-floor level and around which the stairs are wrapped. The stairs provide an ever-changing view as one climbs to the third floor and animate the atrium with the shapes of openings and penetrating forms.

Privacy does not appear to be an issue, since the second-floor master bedroom is largely open to the atrium and a connecting stair reaches across the void to the third-level master bathroom which is also open to the major space. This bathroom leads to an outside basketball court on the roof.

The finishes – a polished-concrete slab, exposed wooden structure, white walls and coloured concrete block – are minimal and elegant.

Levine III Residence (pictured below) stands across the street at 135 Outrigger Mall.

ADDRESS 130 Outrigger Mall, Marina del Rey 90292 [701–J1]
CLIENT Fredric Levine
STRUCTURAL ENGINEER The Office of Gordon Polon
SIZE 3000 square feet (280 square metres)
COST $225,000
ACCESS none

**Marina del Rey**

**Frederick Fisher, Architect 1988**

Marina del Rey

**Frederick Fisher, Architect 1988**

# Angeli Mare

This restaurant is located in a forgettable shopping centre which, given that it has placed parking at the back and put the shops on the sidewalk, is nevertheless better than most. But while the rest of the storefronts remain politely within the plane of the centre's façade, this one pushes out beyond it – an act that seems to have caused the painted-plywood and glass walls to buckle. The door has been split into fragments that hit each other at all angles – as though it were too wide and too high for the space available under the stucco portal.

In the bar, spaces are moulded by suggestion. A long curving panel hangs over the bar area like a protective arm. The buckled wall to the street restrains the seating area, which seems to have spilt out on to the sidewalk. In the restaurant, simple open space is moulded from above by the wave-like curves of the dropped plaster ceiling, seen behind a series of organically formed steel ribs that run against the ceiling and down the back wall. Sitting there is like being inside the ribcage of a great beast. The dining room is brightly lit and on display behind floor-to-ceiling glass. The bar is secreted behind a solid wall that sits on top of a sheet of opaque glass that reveals the patrons inside only from the ankle down.

**Marina del Rey**

ADDRESS 13455 Maxella Avenue, Los Angeles 90292 [672–B6]
CLIENT Evan Kleiman
STRUCTURAL ENGINEER Castillo Miguel
SIZE 4000 square feet (370 square metres)
COST $400,000 (excluding kitchen equipment)
ACCESS open

**Michele Saee 1991**

**Marina del Rey**

**Michele Saee 1991**

# West LA/Westwood/UCLA

**Ove Arup & Partners**

An open-plan workspace for a world-famous group of engineers has been crafted within a renovated 45-year-old warehouse. On entering the offices, twisting stageset-like walls funnel you into the work area beyond, where they continue to soar overhead. The bold design is set within the original space and the exposed bowstring trusses, brick walls, steel columns and wood beams of the original structure read as a voluminous envelope.

The offices occupy two separate volumes linked by a structurally independent chain of rooms. These glass-enclosed 'rooms within a room' are of an aesthetically crude construction and house executive offices, conference rooms and a kitchen. The glass provides acoustic privacy but allows the open quality of the main space to continue.

Parts of the mechanical system have been exposed to celebrate the engineering skill of the client. At the entrance, part of the floor, made of concrete tiles, has been removed to reveal the ducts, cables and conduits that run below. Beside the central conference room, air movement is expressed by rotating fan impellers displayed in glass ducts.

ADDRESS 2440 South Sepulveda Boulevard, Suite 180, Los Angeles 90064 [632–B6]
CLIENT Ove Arup and Partners, California
STRUCTURAL ENGINEER Ove Arup & Partners California
SIZE 14,250 square feet (1300 square metres)
COST $607,000
ACCESS none

West LA/Westwood/UCLA

**Morphosis 1993**

**Morphosis 1993**

**Lowe Residence**

Unusual solutions for earthquake survival and the conservation of natural resources have served as impulses in the design of this striking pair of buildings.

Shock-absorbing devices called 'base isolators' have been set between the structure and the foundations. Corners are supported by visco-damper base isolators (a cylinder within a cylinder, separated by a viscous substance) and the remaining structure rests on 11 smaller units. These German-made devices have been used to absorb ground movement in large European commercial buildings since 1907.

For energy efficiency, interlocking refrigeration panels clad the first floor and end walls of the exposed steel frame. Kalwall panels enclose the upper two floors. The inside faces of these panels and the exposed structure are left visible in the interior.

ADDRESS 1955 1/2 Purdue Avenue, West Los Angeles 90025 [632–A5]
CLIENT David Ming-Li Lowe
STRUCTURAL ENGINEER Philip Ashamallah
SIZE 4770 square feet (443 square metres)
COST $800,000 including land
ACCESS none

**David Ming-Li Lowe, Architect 1993**

**David Ming-Li Lowe, Architect 1993**

# Armand Hammer Museum of Art and Cultural Center

This museum's conception was surrounded by controversy after Armand Hammer broke his 17-year promise to donate his collections to the Los Angeles County Museum of Art and announced plans to build a gallery of his own instead. Yet the Armand Hammer Museum is welcomed as a pleasant place to look at art. There are six gallery spaces – four for the permanent collection and two for temporary exhibitions. The interiors are well proportioned, intimate, minimal and well lit. The rooms are washed with natural light from electronically controlled skylights with artificial light provided for evenings and dark days by concealed fluorescent tubes.

The building itself is less of a success. Clad in alternate bands of grey and white Carrara marble and built on the back of a 1960s' structure occupied by Hammer's Occidental Petroleum Corporation headquarters, the museum has been described as 'a shoe box wearing prison stripes'. The concept of modelling the building on a Renaissance palazzo has resulted in a two–storey mass surrounding a central courtyard. The ground level of the courtyard is framed by inaccessible spaces with the galleries occupying the upper level.

During construction, a law suit was filed by shareholders of Occidental Petroleum objecting to the use of corporate funds to finance this vanity museum. The result was a court settlement that limited the funds the oil company could spend on housing Hammer's $400-million art collection. In consequence, a theatre, library and café have yet to be realised, while cheap and unpleasant materials give the courtyard and upper terraces a commercial feel rather than the intended sense of serenity. A planned pedestrian entrance on Lindbrook Avenue has never been opened.

**Edward Larrabee Barnes 1990**

**Edward Larrabee Barnes 1990**

In March 1994, an arrangement was reached whereby UCLA will take over management of this under-subscribed complex. The uncompleted spaces are to be finished, the Lindbrook Avenue entrance will be opened so that the community has access to the courtyard and an ambitious programme is scheduled to bring life into this mausoleum.

**West LA/Westwood/UCLA**

ADDRESS 10899 Wilshire Boulevard, Los Angeles 90024 [632–B3]
CLIENT Occidental Petroleum Corporation
STRUCTURAL ENGINEER John A Martin & Associates
SIZE 89,400 square feet (8300 square metres)
ACCESS Tuesday to Saturday 11.00–19.00, Sunday 11.00–18.00

**Edward Larrabee Barnes 1990**

West LA/Westwood/UCLA

**Edward Larrabee Barnes 1990**

**Contempo Casuals**

Located on the intersection that marks the heart of Westwood Village, this clothing store occupies a monumental Italian-style building that was once a bank. The original volume has been stripped down to its bones to display the dome over the entrance and the line of heavy trusses that runs the length of the main space. This serves as a backdrop to the dramatic interventions inserted within.

Morphosis has designed a metal hanging system of brackets, racks and shelves that is employed throughout the shop to display the garments for sale. Filling the central space is a massive two-level structure made from rusted steel, wood, perforated-metal panels and sandblasted glass. Typically Morphosian, it is tough but beautiful and serves as a central display area. Sadly, the owners have altered the design significantly and what we see now is not as Morphosis intended.

ADDRESS 1801 Westwood Boulevard, Los Angeles 90024 [632–A3]
CLIENT Michael and Ellion Lewis
STRUCTURAL ENGINEER The Office of Gordon Polon
SIZE 5800 square feet (540 square metres)
ACCESS open

**Morphosis 1987**

**West LA/Westwood/UCLA**

**Morphosis 1987**

# UCLA Gordon and Virginia MacDonald Medical Research Laboratories

The research activities now housed within this decorated shed were previously located in eight different buildings. The programme was to consolidate the functions, create an environment that would facilitate collaboration and provide a flexibility that could accommodate future needs. To accomplish this, the building was designed from the inside out using the same plan for each of the seven floors except the entry level. Work and office spaces are located on the perimeter to gain natural daylight and mechanical and support spaces occupy the central core, with a racetrack corridor for circulation.

The brick elevation makes reference to the surrounding medical buildings as well as to the 1920s' Lombardian Romanesque buildings at the core of the campus. The elevations have been designed to be seen from a courtyard that will be created when a future building sitting between this and Westwood Boulevard is completed. The large ornamental column on Westwood Boulevard and the ramp climbing up to the big archway that enters the colonnade are grand gestures intended to address the campus at large.

ADDRESS UCLA, 405 Hilgard Avenue, Westwood 90024 [632–B2]
CLIENT UCLA School of Medicine
ASSOCIATE ARCHITECT Payette Associates
STRUCTURAL ENGINEER John A Martin & Associates
SIZE 157,450 square feet (14,600 square metres)
COST $47.2 million
ACCESS none

**Venturi, Scott Brown and Associates 1991**

**Venturi, Scott Brown and Associates 1991**

**UCLA Towell Library**

While UCLA's Powell Library is undergoing a five-year seismic upgrading, its books have been moved across campus to a newly erected temporary home. Making no bones about its impermanence, the structure is a tent for technologically sophisticated Bedouin. A skin of coated woven polyester is stretched over curved extruded-aluminium ribs. The office areas are defined by corrugated metal sheeting over wood framing. Glazing is clear and corrugated polycarbonate. As far as possible, the structure has been designed so its various elements can be reused once it is dismantled.

Looking like a hastily erected circus tent or a sinister cocoon pulsing with quiescent life, the structure is satisfyingly obdurate when it comes to declaring its meaning. Nothing seems at rest or in equilibrium. Supposedly neutral technology adopts an air of menace, and a building that should celebrate learning seems instead to question it, or at least its application.

Prepared by the exterior for a dystopian view of the world, it is a surprise to step inside and find an interior that is literally bathed in light. But lest one become complacent, the architects have included an elevator tower that looks disconcertingly like a sentry post at a maximum-security prison. Look closely, however: the more you stare, the more the corrugated-plastic baffle that tops it looks like the crown of the Statue of Liberty. PL

ADDRESS UCLA, 405 Hilgard Avenue, Westwood 90024 [632–B2]
CLIENT UCLA
STRUCTURAL ENGINEER Robert Englekirk Consulting Engineers, Inc
SIZE 43,766 square feet (4066 square metres)
COST $3.5 million
ACCESS open

West LA/Westwood/UCLA

**Hodgetts + Fung Design Associates 1993**

**Hodgetts + Fung Design Associates 1993**

# UCLA Energy Services Facility

In 1987 the University decided to replace its outdated and inefficient network of mechanical and electrical services with a single central plant that would reduce air pollution while supplying steam, chilled water and electricity to the entire campus. To increase efficiency, the University chose to incorporate co-generation which produces additional steam and electricity by recycling waste heat. The design-build team of Parsons Main/Kiewitt with Holt Hinshaw Pfau Jones as the architectural consultants was awarded the commission when they won a limited design competition held by the university.

Co-generation plants work best on a single level, but the 8-acre site was too limited to place all the requirements on one floor. To make the scheme work, Holt Hinshaw Pfau Jones collaborated with the engineers Parsons Main and succeeded in finding a solution that stacks the Co-gen plant on three storeys instead of one. Through the use of similar materials and colour, this massive, well-detailed celebration of technology shows off its industrial components while tying in with the two-storey police station fronting it on Westwood Boulevard. A building such as this is more likely to be built in an industrial or rural area, but finding itself in the middle of a suburban campus, it has respected it context which is predominantly made up of brick-clad medical buildings.

The programme was to provide for chiller and power-generating equipment, offices and workshops. The building is split lengthwise down the middle with the machinery occupying the south side of the structure. A framework of steel stairways and catwalks on the north elevation screens the three levels of inhabited spaces filling that side. In elevation, panels of patterned brickwork clad the ground floor, marking the location of the gas turbine generators and absorption refrigeration chillers. At the upper level, huge, propped metal screens tantalise the observer as they

**Holt Hinshaw Pfau Jones 1994**

**Holt Hinshaw Pfau Jones 1994**

alternately conceal then reveal the heat-recovery steam generators and the cooling towers. At the top, the two stacks stretch heroically to their 125-foot limit.

One might have expected this building's size and function to have a monstrous impact on its surroundings, but instead it has enhanced the environment both architecturally and technolgically.

ADDRESS 405 Hilgard Avenue, Westwood 90024 [632–B2]
CLIENT University of Southern California, Los Angeles
PROJECT ENGINEERS Parsons Main, Inc
GENERAL CONTRACTOR Kiewitt Pacific Co
SIZE 180,000 square feet (16,700 square metres)
COST $180 million including machinery
ACCESS none

**Holt Hinshaw Pfau Jones 1994**

**Holt Hinshaw Pfau Jones 1994**

**UCLA Childcare Center**

High-tech and nature come together in this building to create a charmed setting for the care of children. Sited at the north-west corner of the UCLA campus in an area that was once an orchard, it consists of a central administration block flanked by two independent classroom wings. The U shape formed by these structures cradles the children's outdoor play area, with the fourth side left open to the landscape beyond. This relationship between space and nature is the essence of the scheme. The classrooms are mostly transparent and porches covered by fibreglass panels extend from them into the central U to create protected outdoor play areas.

Once the architects had been commissioned, the clients informed them that the deadline had changed and work had to be completed in four months. They rose to the occasion and the design was done in two weeks, with construction completed three-and-a-half months later. The buildings use a prefabricated system of steel modules infilled with aluminium frames that was developed by the Lees in collaboration with Ove Arup & Partners.

The director is enthusiastic about the idea of the building as a teaching tool. She believes the natural materials help children to understand what buildings are made of and the exposed frame helps them to see how buildings are put together.

ADDRESS UCLA, 405 Hilgard Avenue, Westwood 90024 [632–B2]
CLIENT The Regents of the University of California at Los Angeles
STRUCTURAL ENGINEER Ove Arup & Partners, California
SIZE 10,000 square feet (930 square metres)
COST $2 million (site and building)
ACCESS none

**Office of Charles and Elizabeth Lee – Architects 1988**

West LA/Westwood/UCLA

**Office of Charles and Elizabeth Lee – Architects 1988**

# Culver City

# Michael Ruppert Studio

Taking a cue from Los Angeles' tradition of thematic architecture, this building is designed to communicate emphatically the nature of the work that goes on inside.

The owner is a commercial photographer who shoots products ranging from small objects to cars. The building houses two double-height studios at ground level with offices on the second floor. Ringing a third-level roof terrace are three independent volumes that will contain a client lounge, conference room and additional studio. Elevations are clad in galvanised sheet metal and steel trowel-finish stucco, giving the geometric forms a machine-like aesthetic. References to film and photography abound throughout.

The ratios for 4 x 5 inch transparencies and 35 mm slides inform the window proportions. Corners of the building are capped with galvanised metal triangles that suggest photo mounts. The peel-off cladding is a reference to Polaroid film, which is in constant use. The most obvious reference to the owner's occupation is the giant film cannister on the roof terrace which contains a space from which overhead shots can be made into the studio below.

ADDRESS 12130 Washington Place, Los Angeles 90066 [672–D4]
CLIENT Michael Ruppert
STRUCTURAL ENGINEER Ismail Germiyannoglu
SIZE 15,000 square feet (1400 square metres)
COST $1.5 million
ACCESS none

**Ted Tokio Tanaka Architect 1991**

**Ted Tokio Tanaka Architect 1991**

Culver City

**Tisch-Avnet**

Tisch-Avnet is one of the most refined of the commercial rehabs on which Frank Israel has built his reputation. The basic structure is a four-storey PoMo office block of little interest or distinction. Significant remodelling has been confined to the entrance, lobby and third floor.

A canopy over the doorway is integrated into a towering steel and wood screen that rises the three storeys of the lobby. On the third floor a long, curving, colour-impregnated plaster wall creates a sophisticated ambience within the large reception and circulation area. Perpendicular to this axis, a sheetmetal-clad corridor leads towards a conference room and offices. Without the space to build the freestanding structures he used at Propaganda Films (see page 232) and Bright and Associates (see page 114), Israel has provided more orthodox spaces and corridors that are nevertheless enlivened by curved walls or ceilings.

The high point of this design is the conference room. Small in plan, it rises two storeys to a skylight. Sandblasted-plexiglass screens, canted out from the walls, catch and hold light while seemingly floating above one's head. The ethereal quality of this room proves that Israel's best work is still created with simple materials and novel ideas. PL

ADDRESS 3815 Hughes Avenue, Culver City
90232 [672–G1]
CLIENT Steve Tisch and John Avnet
STRUCTURAL ENGINEER Davis/Fejes
SIZE 25,000 square feet (2300 square metres)
ACCESS none

**Franklin D Israel Design Associates, Inc 1991**

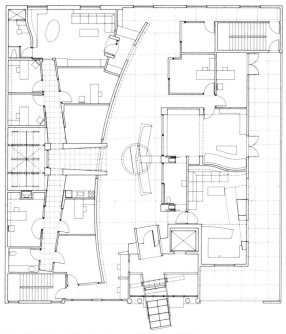

**Franklin D Israel Design Associates, Inc 1991**

**Ince**

Four things connect these three converted warehouses – the same owner, the same architect, the same type of usage (office space for companies working in creative areas) and the same parking lot. They are the first projects collaborated on by Eric Owen Moss and Culver City patron Frederick Norton Smith, a partnership hell-bent on turning east Culver City into LA's new cultural Mecca. It is not certain how much property Smith owns in this part of town nor how far he will run with the same architect. But in addition to Ince and 8522 National Boulevard (see page 164) there are several other collaborations either near completion, under construction or on the drawing boards at Moss' office.

Culver City

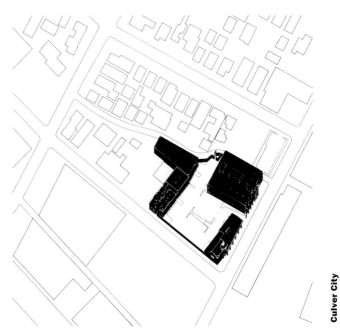

**Culver City**

**Eric Owen Moss Architects 1987–1990**

**Paramount Laundry Building**

This is a renovation of a 20,000-square-foot warehouse built in 1940. Inside, a second floor has been extended so that it lofts into the central, double-height space and a two-part third floor and a new canopy and lobby have been built on to the front elevation. A new vault, adjusted in plan to address the Santa Monica Freeway, penetrates the roof to identify the new elements of the building. Attention-grabbing details refuse to let these additions remain simple.

The columns supporting the exterior canopy are made from sewer pipes filled with concrete. One column bends as a gesture to the parking lot entrance. The stair system sets up a language of contrasts. There are faceted elements juxtaposed against curved elements, balustrades that are solid are clasped to balustrades that are transparent and two sets of stairs wrap around a square form pierced by a circular void.

In the central space, a double row of vitrified clay pipes supports both the lofted second floor addition and the bridge that connects the two sections of the third level. To obtain vertical clearance, the bridge fearlessly cuts through the bottom chord of the existing wooden trusses which are then restructured with steel insertions.

ADDRESS 3960 Ince Boulevard, Culver City 90232
CLIENT Frederick Norton Smith
STRUCTURAL ENGINEER Kurily Szymanski Tchirkow
SIZE 25,395 square feet (2360 square metres)
ACCESS none

**Culver City**

**Eric Owen Moss Architects 1989**

**Eric Owen Moss Architects 1989**

**Culver City**

# Lindblade Tower

Moss aims to rattle one's complacency, twisting things so that the simple becomes quite involved. Here, he manipulates the notions of entrance, solid and void, inside and outside.

A renovation of a warehouse built in the 1940s, the entrance is established by a new tower, its pyramidal roof cut and rotated to orient itself to the freeway. Outside, the tower reads as walls. Inside, the tower is reduced to columns at its corners and the sense of enclosure is unnerved when the roof is removed. A skylight at ceiling level looks through the tower towards the remaining roof frame.

Within the open internal area there are two opposing volumes. One is covered in sheet metal and accommodates bathrooms and mechanical equipment. The other, a courtyard, is clad entirely in glass. One wall rolls up completely to connect inside with outside and small, pivoting windows set into the seamless side walls appear to float in mid air.

The canopy on the front elevation is supported by the same vitrified clay pipes that are used at the Paramount Laundry Building. Wishing to expose the tricks of the trade, the pipes are cut away to reveal their concrete filling.

ADDRESS 3958 Ince Boulevard, Culver City 90232
CLIENT Frederick Norton Smith
STRUCTURAL ENGINEER The Office of Gordon Polon
SIZE 5300 square feet (490 square metres)
ACCESS none

**Culver City**

**Eric Owen Moss Architects 1989**

**Eric Owen Moss Architects 1989**

**Gary Group Office Building**

Within a renovated warehouse, a maze of offices intermingling with open courtyards is set up. These courtyards and some pretty hefty skylights provide natural light for an advertising and promotion agency. Within this labyrinth, two of the spaces are pretty extraordinary. One is a courtyard that contains a fountain where water falls from standard shower heads to slide down the inclined faces of marble sheets and land in a pool at ground level. The second is a conference room. Steel, birch, masonry, plaster and glass are used to structure a very complicated space. Inclined panels suggest an octagon set into a square. Wood legs grow from steel and are stabilised by a steel ring (facets against curves) to support a conical steel and glass skylight.

There are two main elevations. The Lindblade Street elevation is a pierced, inclined masonry wall that leans against an adjoining wall. Sheared signage and elaborate gestures supporting a clock turned 90 degrees serve as ornament. Facing the parking lot is an elevation that expresses the junction of the rebel and the conventionalist. Chains, wheels, cables, bolted acrylic panels, re-bar and stone boxes adorn this façade in a punk fashion – but the boxes are for plants and the re-bar ladders are to grow them on.

**Culver City**

ADDRESS 9046 Lindblade Street, Culver City 90232
CLIENT Frederick Norton Smith
STRUCTURAL ENGINEER Davis Design Group
SIZE 7735 square feet (720 square metres)
ACCESS none

**Eric Owen Moss Architects 1990**

**Eric Owen Moss Architects 1990**

# 8522 National Boulevard

This project is a conversion of an existing building made up of five adjoining warehouses built between the 1920s and the 1940s. There was no strategy for the additions – new space was just created as it was needed. Now, the building has been given a sense of clarity and cohesion.

The solution adds semi-public space in the form of an internal street, toplit through a continuous lantern, that follows the L-shaped form of the building with the commercial space on either side. The entry has been articulated by stretching a steel canopy across the street elevation and propping it on struts that extend from the existing wall. An elliptical entry court has been cut into the original building and into the canopy, exposing a piece of the column-and-truss system that runs down the centre of the internal street and gives it its most identifiable characteristic.

The walls to the street are made as a three-layer sandwich, with each layer setting its own rhythm. One layer is a series of framed rectangular openings (painted drywall), the next is a series of wider arches (speckled blue plaster) and the third a glass wall.

Where the two arms of the internal street meet, an elliptical curve inflates the intersection, forming a secondary lobby. From here, the walkway is narrowed and terminates at a large conference room intended initially to be shared by all tenants, but now privately held by the offices directly opposite.

The conference room is essentially a rectangular masonry box with an elliptical cone made of birch plywood set within it. This wooden lining gives the room a polished finish, but this is subverted by large plywood cut-outs which reveal portions of the original blockwork and structural studwork.

In designing the interiors of the private space, Eric Moss repeats a theme. The private offices are predominantly rectilinear spaces into which

**Culver City**

**Eric Owen Moss Architects 1990**

a disruptive central piece has been dropped. A pentagonal library pushes its irregular strandboard-clad walls into the easiness of the white plastered rooms surrounding it in the Qualitative Research Center. In Goalen a major skylit intersection is created. Thick walls surround the space and play a game: if they are facetted on the inside they are curved on the outside, and *vice versa*. In Scott Mednick Associates, the imposition hangs above the major work space where a web of curving steel ribs, lights, electrical conduits, skylights and ducts creates a sense of order rather than disruption.

**Culver City**

ADDRESS 8522 National Boulevard, Culver City 90232 [632–G7]
CLIENT Frederick Norton Smith
STRUCTURAL ENGINEER The Office of Gordon Polon
SIZE 53,940 square feet (5000 square metres)
ACCESS entry and internal street only

**Eric Owen Moss Architects 1990**

**Eric Owen Moss Architects 1990**

# Beverly Hills/Bel Air

**Art Pavilion**

This freestanding pavilion is situated on an 8-acre site in an exclusive residential area beside a large Mediterranean-style home that was built in the early 1920s and is attributed to Wallace Neff. Its general air of restraint allows the focus to fall on the important collection of Abstract Expressionist art displayed inside.

The intention for the exterior was to complement the prevailing Mediterranean style of the homes in the area, but not too literally. The lower walls are clad in stucco to match the existing house, with the upper walls clad in both fibreglass-reinforced concrete and in glass panels set in mahogany frames.

The top floor is given over to a gallery with a 28-foot-high ceiling supported by massive timber trusses. Large Wrightian corner windows provide rhythmic breaks between the canvases and let in views of trees and sky. Movable walls regulate the light and allow the room to function as a reception or lecture space. The two-storey base contains additional gallery space, archive, guest quarters, conservation laboratory and loggia.

Where the opportunity has arisen, Israel has done his own sculpting. An elegant floating steel stair connects the two upper floors and a mahogany, steel and marble bar/storage unit hovers above the stairwell. Outside, rain scuppers and the cap to an independent elevator evoke samurai while the loggia is surrounded by an elaborate steel railing. The most striking feature of all is the giant balcony with canopy that hangs over the garden side of the building. Constructed of steel and wood, it is boat shaped and looks as though it is being lifted up from the garden.

ADDRESS 275 North Carolwood Drive, Bel Air 90077 [592–C6]
STRUCTURAL ENGINEER Davis/Fejes
ACCESS none

**Franklin D Israel Design Associates Inc 1991**

**Franklin D Israel Design Associates Inc 1991**

# Click Model Management and Flick Agency

An ocean theme (inspired by the street name?) determines the character of the three dynamic contrasting forms that push themselves into a narrow, glass-enclosed space. A gently curving and canting wall (the ship) is linked by a second-level bridge (the gangplank) to a pink stucco wall (the dock). The tight canyon that remains between these volumes links the front lobby to a central open space with an egg-shaped volume at the back. These forms contain offices, a conference room and services and are all clad in different materials to emphasise their uniqueness. Executive desks shaped like shark fins and a conference table that looks like a surfboard continue the ocean theme in the interior.

Situated on a narrow back street, this double-height office sits above enclosed parking. The street-level elevation is clad in metal and, in accordance with the high visibility of the business, the upper level is transparent, displaying the activity within.

ADDRESS 9057 Nemo Street, West Hollywood 90069 [592–H7]
CLIENT Click Model Management
STRUCTURAL ENGINEER Niver Engineering
SIZE 5900 square feet (550 square metres)
COST $683,625
ACCESS by appointment; telephone (310) 247 1777

**Beverly Hills/Bel Air**

**Hodgetts + Fung Design Associates 1992**

**Hodgetts + Fung Design Associates 1992**

**Beverly Hills Civic Center**

The winning scheme in an invited design competition, the Civic Center's realisation fails to live up to the architects' intentions. It was hoped that a public life similar to that found in many European cities would be provided for, but budgetary cut-backs and the failure of the municipality to adhere to the architects' vision led to a scheme which is ultimately a disappointment.

Plans to expand the existing civic centre, whose focus was the City Hall built by William J Gage in 1932, were approved in the 1980s. The programme called for the addition of a fire station, a parking structure, a police station and major expansion of the existing library. Participants were asked to suggest additional community facilities, and this team proposed a theatre, a cafeteria and an art gallery. In the design solution, a diagonal chain of elliptical courtyards running from the south-west corner of the site to the north-east corner was inserted between the buildings. This pedestrian environment has balconies, arcades and open circulation corridors at the upper levels and planted courtyards below. A height limit of 40 feet was established to allow the City Hall to dominate and the architects decided to draw on its Spanish-colonial appearance and use its rhythmic bay system throughout the new scheme.

Financial decisions undermined the success of this project. After the theatre design was completed and a budget set, the bids were considered too expensive and the architects were asked to redesign the space as a parking lot for the library. The cafeteria was supposed to face the art gallery across the courtyard, but both of these were cancelled and the art gallery's space is now used for mechanical equipment for the police station. Water features in the courtyards and cascading water at the south-west entrance were also dropped.

As built, there are not even benches in the courtyards that might give

**Charles Moore and the Urban Innovations Group 1990**

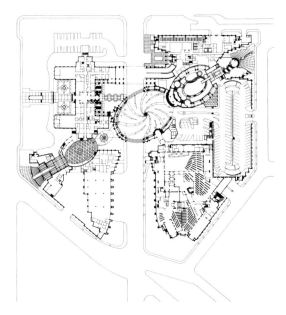

**Charles Moore and the Urban Innovations Group 1990**

a reason for lingering and one wonders why anyone might want to walk through these spaces at all. The police station, library and fire station are not accessed from the courtyards so one has to leave them to search for the entries.

The architects' vision of providing a place for a rich public life has been reduced beyond recognition. The grand staircase at the corner of Burton Way and Crescent Drive succeeds as an invitation to enter this sequence of spaces, but ultimately leads one through an empty experience.

**Beverly Hills/Bel Air**

ADDRESS site bounded by Crescent Drive, Santa Monica Boulevard, Civic Center Drive and Burton Way, Beverly Hills 90210 [632–G1]
CLIENT City of Beverly Hills
STRUCTURAL ENGINEER Albert C Martin and Associates
ACCESS open

**Charles Moore and the Urban Innovations Group 1990**

**Charles Moore and the Urban Innovations Group 1990**

# Virgin Records

Situated off the street, within the interior of a city block, a renovated warehouse contains the American offices of Virgin Records. A bulging, red stucco wall, punctured to allow glimpses of a private desert garden, masks the original elevation. The entrance is marked by a translucent canopy in the form of a flat v hanging from a single line of steel columns.

Inside, the front of the building is occupied by a suite of business offices behind a canting green plaster wall. In the back, private offices lining two parallel corridors provide accommodation for the creative staff.

A short axis from the entrance lobby intersects with a wide cross-axis that provides space for parties and performances. An amphitheatre occupies a large part of it and wood and steel braces supporting a continuous length of back-lit fibreglass create a dramatic backdrop.

The ceiling is cluttered with exposed structure and services. Wood beams, conduits, air-conditioning and heating vents, pipes, steel crossbars, snaking catwalks holding electric cables and hanging task lighting all serve as a reminder of what it might look like if one could see the sounds that travel the airwaves.

ADDRESS 338 North Foothill Road, Beverly Hills 90210 [592–G1]
CLIENT Virgin Records America, Inc
STRUCTURAL ENGINEER Stephen Perlof
SIZE 28,000 square feet (2600 square metres)
ACCESS none

**Franklin D Israel Design Associates Inc 1991**

**Franklin D Israel Design Associates Inc 1991**

# Maple Drive

Sited in a standard commercial building in a space with a rigid structural grid and fixed ceiling heights, this restaurant set its architects the challenge of making its vast area as intimate as possible. The solution is provided by some neat spatial manœuvres and an exciting array of ceiling treatments and lighting designs.

There are five distinct spaces – the bar, main dining room, oyster bar, dining terrace and private dining room. The bar is lit primarily by a dropped steel tartan grid that grips halogen spots. Other sections are differentiated either by painting the ceiling black or leaving it bare, while a low soffit defines the row of banquettes. In the main dining room a coffered grid is established which is edge lit by concealed cold-cathode tubes. An exuberant steel fixture with suspended halogen spots lights the oyster bar.

There is a wide range of materials – granite, grey cement plaster, copper beams, slate, maple, burnished stainless steel and rusted-steel sections in the light fixtures.

Each patron is displayed as she/he descends the tapering ramp that links the bar and dining room, and then enjoys an intimacy and quiet that is unlike most other fashionable restaurants.

ADDRESS 345 North Maple Drive, Beverly Hills 90210 [632–G2]
CLIENT Main Course Management
STRUCTURAL ENGINEER KPFF
SIZE 9000 square feet (840 square metres)
COST $2.9 million
ACCESS open

**L Anthony Greenberg AIA 1989**

**L Anthony Greenberg AIA 1989**

**Creative Artists Agency**

Unusually well detailed for Los Angeles, and evidently from a design tradition quite different to the indigenous, I M Pei's sophisticated and quietly expensive building for Mike Ovitz nevertheless fits well into this busy Beverly Hills intersection. Rounding the corner from Wilshire Boulevard on to Little Santa Monica at the same three-storey height as its bland neighbour, a visor of mirrored glass cantilevers out from a curving wall of Onda Marina travertine. Between this and a second volume, also curved, a glass-walled entryway leads into a 56-foot-high atrium overlooked by balconies and walkways. Acres of travertine cover the walls and floor, leaving the space cool and airy and, because of the wonderful quality of the light and the pleasing proportions, unexpectedly comfortable. A large ficus tree softens the edges and a Lichtenstein and grouping of Breuer chairs tell you that the place belongs to someone who knows his way around MOMA.

If it were not for the alienating effect of the reflective glass, this would be a more successful building. PL

ADDRESS 9830 Wilshire Boulevard, Beverly Hills 90212 [632–G2]
CLIENT Creative Artists Agency
STRUCTURAL ENGINEER Leslie E Robertson Associates, New York;
John A Martin & Associates, Los Angeles
SIZE 26,162 square feet (2430 square metres) site area; 75,000 square feet (7000 square metres) gross building area
ACCESS none

Beverly Hills/Bel Air

**Pei Cobb Freed & Partners Architects 1989**

Beverly Hills/Bel Air

**Pei Cobb Freed & Partners Architects 1989**

# 2 Rodeo Drive

Not since Malibu's J Paul Getty Museum has Los Angeles seen such lavish pastiche. Located on the retail street that claims to be the most expensive in the world, this shopping centre spells 'class'. To lure shoppers in, Hollywood versions of a European shopping street, public square and the Spanish Steps in Rome have been built over a subterranean parking lot. The development has shop fronts on Wilshire Boulevard and Rodeo Drive and a new cobble pedestrian street, Via Rodeo, that bisects the site. The project contains high-end retail and *haute couture* outlets behind individually designed two- and three-storey elevations that share a common structurally considered steel framework. Details are so careful that Walt Disney could have commissioned it.

Not to be missed is the complementary valet parking lot below. Continuing the experience of lavish surroundings, this space has been finished to a level appropriate for human habitation. The walls, ceiling and columns are plaster coated and painted a rose-tinted white; lighting is indirect. Cobblestones and a petite Victorian street lamp serve as reminders that this is indeed a place for cars.

ADDRESS 2 Rodeo Drive, Beverly Hills 90210 [632–G2]
CLIENT Doug Stitzel
STRUCTURAL ENGINEER HKA Consulting Engineers
SIZE 136,000 square feet (12,600 square metres) of retail space over garage parking for 600 cars
ACCESS open

**Enzo Zicenzino/Kaplan McLaughlin Diaz 1990**

**Enzo Zicenzino/Kaplan McLaughlin Diaz 1990**

# Kate Mantilini

Kate Mantilini is a building within a building. The new structure, wrapped in solid plaster walls, is set within the remaining thin steel frame of the building that previously occupied the site. The interior is a large, regularly shaped courtyard-like space enlivened both by incisions and intrusions. Plastered *poché* walls enclose the kitchen on one side and a canting plaster wall shelters the private booths opposite. These create a frame for the central space with its gridded stone floor and night-sky ceiling of black acoustical tiles with a lighting plan defined by the owner's zodiac sign.

There are two focal elements. One is a large mural of boxers by John Wehrle which hangs above the counter area. This is a reference to the restaurant's namesake, who was a female boxing promoter in the 1940s (and the mistress of the present owner's uncle). The second is the conceptual orrery – a large sculptural piece made up of elements of the building (a fragment of the mural, steelwork, posts and lintels) – that is meant to describe the space within which it stands. At its base, a needle seems to be drawing an image of the building – suggesting that it is returning to its status as a drawing.

ADDRESS 9101 Wilshire Boulevard, Beverly Hills 90210 [632–G2]
CLIENT Marilyn Lewis
STRUCTURAL ENGINEER Erdelyi/Mezey Associates
SIZE 6400 square feet (600 square metres)
COST $1.5 million (excluding kitchen equipment)
ACCESS open

Beverly Hills/Bel Air

**Morphosis 1987**

**Morphosis 1987**

**ICM Building**

The ICM Building and the nearby Foothill Thrift and Loan (see page 190) started life as a development by the now-departed Columbia Savings and Loan. The brief called for a headquarters building for the S and L and two speculative office buildings, all to be located within a few blocks of each other on the south side of Wilshire Boulevard in Beverly Hills.

The proximity of the sites and their location on such a major thoroughfare lead to the conceptualisation of the three as related structures, almost as fragments of one building, united stylistically but distinguished by differences in detailing, that would reveal themselves to motorists as strongly articulated horizontal presences, mirroring the flow of the street. The very act of driving down the boulevard would then bring the structures together. Although only two of the three were built, the intention has survived.

The three-storey ICM Building – the larger of the two and designed to be the middle of the three – occupies an entire block. Its street façade is made up of a number of receding planes. The primary plane is an elevated wall of limestone panels into which window openings have been cut. This is supported by a steel framework which overlays a plane of glasswork. A courtyard is cut into the central section of the building and a steel structure marks the entrance by dividing the façade. Against all the odds, on the street the ICM Building is dour and vaguely disturbing. One is left with a feeling that the building is too clever for its own good. PL

ADDRESS 8942 Wilshire Boulevard, Beverly Hills 90211 [632–H2]
CLIENT Columbia Savings and Loan
STRUCTURAL ENGINEER Skidmore Owings & Merrill, Inc
SIZE 82,000 square feet (7600 square metres)
ACCESS none

**Richard Keating/Skidmore, Owings & Merrill, Inc 1990**

**Richard Keating/Skidmore, Owings & Merrill, Inc 1990**

**Foothill Thrift and Loan**

The Foothill Thrift and Loan lies to the west of the ICM Building (see page 188) on Wilshire Boulevard and explores the themes developed in that structure. The same layering exists in the façade, the same broken rhythmns and explorations of excavated space, the same attention to detail and careful engineering of decorative elements, and the same plush interior design. Unfortunately, there is also the same nagging feeling that this is an intellectual and stylistic exercise in deconstruction rather than anything heartfelt. PL

ADDRESS 8942 Wilshire Boulevard, Beverly Hills 90211 [632–G2]
CLIENT Columbia Savings and Loan
STRUCTURAL ENGINEER Skidmore Owings & Merrill, Inc
SIZE 56,000 square feet (5200 square metres)
ACCESS none

**Richard Keating/Skidmore, Owings & Merrill, Inc 1989**

**Richard Keating/Skidmore, Owings & Merrill, Inc 1989**

**Bank of America**

Situated at a busy intersection, this three-storey speculative commercial building is divided into two volumes, each with its own identity. The two street elevations of the smaller volume are green with square windows within a large-scale steel frame. The alternate bands of black and silver glass that clad three sides of the larger volume make it look more two dimensional. The fourth side (and front elevation) is an ominous curved black wall that appears solid but is clad in horizontal bands of black granite and black glass. Passing behind this wall, one enters the triple-height lobby that connects the two volumes.

Inside, the chill of the outer elevations dissipates. The inner walls are clad in stained-plywood panels with large windows cut into them from the commercial spaces. Three giant elliptical columns wrapped in aluminium dominate the space. The white plaster ceiling is artfully splattered with down lights, services and circular skylights.

ADDRESS 8750 Wilshire Boulevard, Beverly Hills 90211 [632–G2]
CLIENT Amir Development Company
STRUCTURAL ENGINEER Ertzan Associates, Inc
SIZE 130,000 square feet (12,000 square metres)
COST $10 million
ACCESS open

**Arquitectonica 1991**

**Arquitectonica 1991**

# Wosk Residence

A blue-domed kitchen, a greenhouse dining room, blue-tile fish scales cladding a corner chimney, a ziggurat coated with gold auto-body paint for a den, a vaulted corrugated-aluminium shed for a studio and a black granite baldachino capping the internal stair collide to create a miniature city on the fourth floor of this pink apartment building. Surprisingly, the interior space is simple, continuous and expansive.

From the inside, one can view the city as well as most of the exterior elements.

**Beverly Hills/Bel Air**

ADDRESS 440 South Roxbury Drive, Beverly Hills 90210 [632–F3]
CLIENT Miriam Wosk
STRUCTURAL ENGINEER Kurily Szymanski Tchirkow
ACCESS none

**Frank O Gehry and Associates 1984**

**Beverly Hills/Bel Air**

**Frank O Gehry and Associates 1984**

# Cedars-Sinai Comprehensive Cancer Center

Located in a precinct known mostly for its architectural horrors, this spectacular building is an outpatient facility providing 24-hour treatment for cancer patients. The first such centre, and intended as a flagship, it offers diagnosis, treatment and counselling within a single setting. The building is complex, rich in detail and has a high surprising quality of natural and indirect light. Focus is directed towards structural expression and self-references that contribute to making patients, staff and visitors aware of their environment.

The predominantly underground structure is pressed against three existing medical buildings on the north-east corner of the 1.5 million-square-foot Cedars-Sinai Hospital site. The only element immediately visible is the pavilion-like entrance wing clad in red Indian sandstone that sits on the edge of a pre-existing parking lot.

One enters the building via a crisp, white corridor lined on one side by a reception counter and on the other by benches. At the end of the corridor a large opening looks down to the main patient level and waiting area set 24 feet below grade and standing 45 feet high. The long space is lit by a half-barrel-vault-skylight and is framed by layered walls. The focal element is a 24-foot-high structure made of steel and wood which supports a 'tree of life' positioned at actual ground level.

This is one of two semi-public spaces. The second is the chemotherapy atrium. A vaulted Kalwall skylight bathes the space with translucent light. The layered wall surfaces are cut with wide openings giving access to the individual treatment rooms which run around the perimeter. Wall fixtures carry indirect night lighting and windows provide views outside.

The subterranean location was determined by the necessity for a direct

**Morphosis 1988**

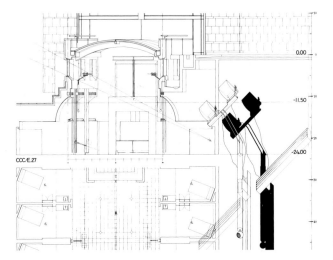

CCC/E.27

0.00

-11.50

-24.00

**Morphosis 1988**

link with the radiation therapy department on the basement level of Cedars-Sinai. The long corridor making that connection between the two is animated by a steady pulse created by layered walls, repeated geometric floor patterns, a curved soffit that provides indirect lighting around its edges and mechanistic wall and ceiling fixtures. The displays of Grant Mudford's black-and-white construction photographs and Morphosis' own colour renderings at either end of the hall transform this space into an art gallery.

ADDRESS 8700 Beverly Boulevard, West Hollywood 90048 [632–J1]
CLIENT Dr Bernard Salick, Salick Health Care, Inc
ASSOCIATE ARCHITECTS Gruen Associates
STRUCTURAL ENGINEER Kurily Szymanski Tchirkow
SIZE 53,000 square feet (4900 square metres)
ACCESS none

**Morphosis 1988**

**Morphosis 1988**

**Beverly Hills/Bel Air**

# Salick Health Care Corporate Headquarters

Salick has twice set challenging design tasks for Morphosis. The Cedars-Sinai Comprehensive Cancer Center (see page 196) had to be accommodated predominantly below ground level; only the entrance pavilion and gallery skylights are expressed above ground level. Here, Salick's head office was to be housed in a bland six-storey 1960s' building. Morphosis was asked to renovate the building while preserving the existing structure and mechanical core.

Through ingenious manipulation of the new elevations, an uneventful building has been given volumetric contrast and surface variation. The original box has been divided in two and each part has been clad in distinctive skins.

The east side achieves a transparency that might seem impossible given Los Angeles' strict energy-conservation codes. Solarflex, a new glass developed by Monsanto for the automobile industry, was used. It is clear, but has the shading and insulating qualities of tinted glass.

In contrast, the west side has been designed as a light-absorbent black box, using a fritted, tinted glass. On the south-facing principal elevation the floor slabs have been notched between the two boxes and a vertical slot has been made, creating the impression that the black box is separate from the rest of the building.

Vertical contrast and a dignified front are provided by the granite face on the south elevation. This starts at street level (the two glass boxes hover above two levels of screened parking) and continues above the roof, propped like a billboard to mask the mechanical penthouse behind.

Inside, the most striking spaces are the two primary public areas at the ground-level entry and the sixth-floor reception space. The most commonly used access to the building is directly from the parking levels

**Morphosis 1991**

Beverly Hills/Bel Air

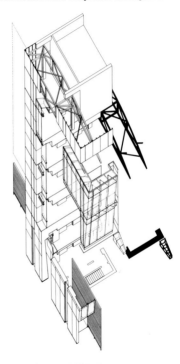

**Morphosis 1991**

into the double-volume lobby. However, pedestrians have been provided with a dramatic entry. One enters from the side into a high, thin sliver of space that seems to have been pulled away from the building. Specially commissioned art transforms it into a gallery. The main reception area on the top floor is wrapped in glass, allowing for panoramic views of Los Angeles and the glass wall on the east end cants outward and seems to project one over Beverly Boulevard.

This triumph of innovative renovation should encourage new thinking about the possibilities of re-using existing building stock.

**Beverly Hills/Bel Air**

ADDRESS 8201 Beverly Boulevard, Los Angeles 90048 [633–A1]
CLIENT Salick Health Care, Inc
STRUCTURAL ENGINEER BP Consulting Engineers
SIZE 36,000 square feet (3300 square metres)
ACCESS none

**Morphosis 1991**

**Morphosis 1991**

# Mid Wilshire to Koreatown

# LACMA: Robert O Anderson Building

The setting for the expansion of LACMA was an uninspired sub-Lincoln Center complex of three buildings around a formal courtyard, designed by William Pereira and completed in 1965. HHPA's answer to the questions of how to add significant space to the museum and how to give it a new identity was to create an infill building that maintains the autonomy of the existing structures while filling most of the courtyard space and creates a bold new public face on Wilshire Boulevard.

Buff-coloured Minnesota limestone, glass block and bands of glazed green terra cotta form an abstract composition that makes reference to Pereira's buildings and to the Art Deco and Art Moderne history of the area. A monumental but undecorated entrance portal, 50 feet wide and 52 feet high, is cut out of the façade and opens on to a high, narrow stairway bounded on one side by the billowing white 4 by 8 foot porcelain-enamelled panels that sheathe the sides of the new building, and on the other by a line of 70-foot-high glazed-terra-cotta-clad columns and a four-tiered waterfall. A partial roof of translucent Kalwall panels and glass offers some protection from the elements while maintaining the feeling of an open space.

Following the stairs upwards, one arrives in the new HHPA-designed Times Mirror Central Court. Also partially covered, this houses information- and ticket-booths and opens on to the four main structures; as well as leading to the more recently completed Japanese Pavilion (see page 210).

The admirable decision to treat the programme as an opportunity to mirror the urban context by dealing in fragments, unexpected juxtapositions and a form of urban archaeology unfortunately succeeds in its more limited objectives while failing at its broader task. Though an enormously photogenic building, particularly when the quilted-enamel panels

**Hardy Holzman Pfeiffer Associates 1986**

**Hardy Holzman Pfeiffer Associates 1986**

are abstracted, the experience of being there is less pleasant. Open spaces that should give form to the overall composition are cramped and claustrophobic, better at engendering urban anxiety than any form of transcendence. It is a relief to get inside the galleries, although these are serviceable at best.

The friendliest entrance, and ironically the one that shows the complex off to its best advantage, is a service ramp into the back of the courtyard from the inexplicably ignored Hancock Park/La Brea Tar Pits. PL

**Mid Wilshire to Koreatown**

ADDRESS 5905 Wilshire Boulevard, Los Angeles 90036 [633–B2]
STRUCTURAL ENGINEER S B Barnes
SIZE Robert O Anderson Building 115,000 square feet (10,700 square metres); Times Mirror Central Court 40,000 square feet (3700 square metres)
COST $35.3 million
ACCESS open

**Hardy Holzman Pfeiffer Associates 1986**

**Hardy Holzman Pfeiffer Associates 1986**

**LACMA Pavilion for Japanese Art**

Part of LACMA's expansion programme, the Pavilion for Japanese Art was designed by Bruce Goff and completed after his death by Bart Prince. An exuberant, inventive and idiosyncratic meditation on Orientalism, the appropriately exotic structure sometimes seems closer to the Klingon Empire than to the Japanese Empire.

Linked to the dreary Times Mirror Central Court (see page 206) by a curving elevated walkway and surrounded by a pleasing but little-used Japanese garden, in plan the pavilion resembles a stylised squid. Two large, circular, reinforced-concrete towers, clad in Utah green quartz aggregate and joined by an exterior bridge, house the stairs and elevators. Six more columns support two triangles of bowed and pointed box beams from which the roofs are suspended by cables. Pale green stucco-work curves organically around the structure as walls, stairs and walkways. In an attempt to evoke the look and light of *shoji* screens, Kalwall panels of varying sizes angle out from the face of the building. Although they manage to create a softly lit internal space, they remain disappointingly two dimensional and disturbingly artificial.

Inside the calm and quiet main gallery, a Guggenheim-like ramp snakes from the elevator-accessed second floor down to the basement where a series of black-tiled water-filled pools flow one into another. The ramp terminates disconcertingly in a multiplex-like tunnel that leads to the bathrooms, forcing one to double back to find the exit. PL

ADDRESS LACMA, 5905 Wilshire Boulevard, Los Angeles 90036 [633–B2]
STRUCTURAL ENGINEER August Mosimann
SIZE 32,100 square feet (3000 square metres)
COST $12.5 million
ACCESS open

**Bruce Goff/Bart Prince 1988**

# Campanile

This restaurant is located in an existing structure built by Lita Grey Chaplin, wife of Charlie Chaplin, in 1926. Considered of historical significance, the existing decorative details have been conserved and the new design responds to the original character while successfully avoiding pastiche. The resuit is a vibrant set of spaces that continually play off notions of inside and outside.

Dining takes place in a linear set of rooms and mezzanines, but the most dynamic spaces are in the existing courtyard which has been enclosed and divided into two areas. The first is an open-air space which the bar opens on to and the second is a long, tightly packed, skylit dining room. Schweitzer BIM also designed and had manufactured the bar stools and light fixtures.

At 180 South La Brea Avenue is City Restaurant, also designed by Josh Schweitzer with David Kellen.

ADDRESS 624 South La Brea Avenue, Los Angeles 90036 [633–D2]
CLIENTS Mark Peel and Nancy Siverton
STRUCTURAL ENGINEER Decoma Engineers
SIZE 10,000 square feet (930 square metres)
ACCESS restaurant hours

**Schweitzer BIM 1988**

**Schweitzer BIM 1988**

# Aloha

On a large corner site in a tough area characterised by a mix of commercial and residential buildings, Josh Schweitzer has built an oasis for himself and his family in what was the Aloha swim school. This is a work in progress, where additional buildings are added as the need arises. Seclusion and privacy are preserved behind the surrounding avocado green wall and the top of a 35-year-old yucca plant is the only element visible from the street.

The bi-level site is dominated by the huge swimming pool, with living quarters accommodated in three separate structures around it. The original changing rooms have been converted into the main living spaces, which are open plan and entirely glazed to the pool view. Two new structures have been added on the top level: one houses a bedroom, the other is a studio which has metamorphosed into a child's bedroom. Plywood clad with canting walls, this studio is the most publicised part of the scheme and in photographs it looks like a small, shed-like building. Typical of Schweitzer's play with form and scale, it is really twice that size.

Circulation between the buildings is outside and unprotected, celebrating the idyllic Southern California climate and exploiting the atypical estate-like nature of the site.

ADDRESS 5243 West Washington Boulevard, Los Angeles 90016 [633–C5]
CLIENTS Josh Schweitzer and Mary Sue Milliken
STRUCTURAL ENGINEER Davis Design
SIZE 10,000 square feet (930 square metres)
ACCESS none

**Schweitzer BIM 1986–**

**Schweitzer BIM 1986–**

**Kentucky Fried Chicken**

When Grinstein/Daniels' KFC was praised in *The Los Angeles Times*, a local resident wrote in to castigate the journalist responsible, suggesting that if they had to drive past the structure each day, their opinion might be different. It is an extraordinary idea that anyone would rather see the traditional KFC logo of Colonel Saunders rotating on the side of an enormous red-striped bucket, than perched on top of this imposing monument to fast food.

What no doubt upset the letter-writer was the sheer size of the structure, the corrugated-steel cladding that covers one wall and the apparently arbitrary inclusion of fins on the front elevation and triangular steel plates on the main stuccoed tower – topped, of course, by the ubiquitous, but stationary, Colonel. Viewed from the street, the effect is of a neo-Constructivist collage.

The architects have made the most of a small site, reducing the building's footprint to a minimum to provide a reasonable number of off-street parking spaces. Food service is on the ground floor, with the soaringly high-ceilinged eating area above. An unusually humane space for the world of fast food, it is filled with light from an enormous L-shaped glass wall that opens out on to a balcony area. The steel triangles that appear so enigmatic from the exterior are revealed from inside to be functional baffles designed to deflect sunlight from a window on the west face. PL

ADDRESS 340 North Western Avenue, Los Angeles 90004 [593–H7]
CLIENT Jack Wilke
STRUCTURAL ENGINEER Erdelyi/Mezey Associates
SIZE 3300 square feet (300 square metres)
COST $550,000
ACCESS open

**Grinstein/Daniels Architects 1989**

**Grinstein/Daniels Architects 1989**

**686 Saint Andrew's Place**

This refurbishment of the façade of an existing apartment block was the first exploration of the 'Ham and Swiss' building type Kanner Architects went on to refine in the Harvard Apartments (see page 222). Distinctive elements of LA's indigenous architecture of the 1930s and 1950s are reinterpreted and reconfigured. It is tempting to see a ghostly echo of the Pan Pacific Auditorium's streamline Moderne pylons in the entryway, and there is no doubting the debt the block's strong visual identity owes 1950s' roadside architecture.

Peppered with circular cut-outs – some windows, some merely indents – walls with a harlequin pattern of white and pale blue diamonds are sandwiched between corner elements of pale yellow that angle outwards towards the street. A tower in the middle of the façade signals the entrance: a passageway through the building to a small private courtyard from which the apartments are accessed. Individual garages line the ground-floor level, facing the street.

Cheap aluminium windows somewhat diminish the effect of a design carried out with brio on an extraordinarily slim budget. PL

ADDRESS 686 South Saint Andrew's Place, Los Angeles 90010 [633–H2]
CLIENT Jordan Ostrow
STRUCTURAL ENGINEER Jun Chung
COST $75,000
ACCESS none

**Kanner Architects 1988**

**Kanner Architects 1988**

# Atlas

Located in the Pellissier Building, better known as the Wiltern, Atlas makes no overt reference to its historic setting. But in following its own course, the restaurant and bar nevertheless manages to create an ambience that is not too dissimilar from that of a 1930s' speakeasy.

Entering through mundane glass and aluminium doors, you are confronted by a spiky metal screen that evokes leaping flames or the pointed leaves of the succulent plant sansevieria. A baroque sofa and chairs covered in imitation leopardskin stand close to the *maître d*'s console. The procession is completed as you are led through swagged velvet curtains into the main dining area. Quiet at lunchtime, Atlas is more animated in the evening, when salsa and jazz bands perform.

The large, high space has been stripped back to a shell and then simply divided by enormous bent-metal screens that depict some of the mythological Atlas's endeavours. Effectively breaking the space into intimate areas, the screens also provide a powerful visual focus, allowing the rest of the décor to be kept as simple as possible. There is a small stage at one end of the dining area, and the bar and kitchen that line two of the walls can be glimpsed through the screens. Hints at a more opulent style create a tone of stripped grandeur – and we may have to thank the minuscule budget for the fact that these remain hints. PL

ADDRESS 3760 Wilshire Boulevard, Los Angeles 90010 [633–H2]
METALWORK Joshua Triliegi
SIZE 3500 square feet (325 square metres)
ACCESS open

**Ron Meyers 1989**

**Ron Meyers 1989**

**Harvard Apartments**

Severe Modernism meets 1950s' Googie in a literal and metaphorical sandwich. Moving on from the Saint Andrew's Place apartments (see page 212), this block really is, as the architects say, 'a ham and Swiss-cheese sandwich of white bread Modernism with a filling of LA funk.' Rigid geometries of white stucco front a yellow slice of 'Swiss', complete with circular cut-outs, that in turn overlays a red segment of 'ham'. White corresponds to living areas, yellow to bathrooms and red to circulation.

Better detailed than the Saint Andrew's Place apartments, this building combines fun and functionalism with a strong sculptural presence. Given its location in the heart of Koreatown, it also stands as a metaphor for racial harmony. PL

ADDRESS 901 South Harvard Boulevard, Los Angeles 90006 [633-J3]
CLIENT Jordan Ostrow
STRUCTURAL ENGINEER Jun Chung
SIZE 13 units; 16,880 square feet (1570 square metres)
COST $600,000
ACCESS none

**Kanner Architects 1992**

Mid Wilshire to Koreatown

**Kanner Architects 1992**

**Shatto Recreation Center**

Set within a public park, this rectangular masonry box houses a gymnasium and community centre. But this is no ordinary box – Steven Ehrlich has collaborated with artist Ed Moses to design a sensuously patterned and textured wall from three different kinds of concrete block with a freely curving, metal-clad roof. In contrast to the warmth of the elevations, a triangular metal-clad canopy marks the entrance.

Likened to a whale, this centre is humane and dignified and it is one of Steven Ehrlich's best buildings in Los Angeles.

ADDRESS 3191 West 4th Street, Los Angeles 90020 [634–C2]
CLIENT City of Los Angeles Department of Recreation and Parks
STRUCTURAL ENGINEER Stephen Perloff
SIZE 12,000 square feet (1000 square metres)
COST $1.8 million
ACCESS open

**Steven Ehrlich Architects 1991**

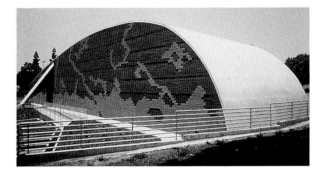

**Steven Ehrlich Architects 1991**

# West Hollywood/Hollywood/
# Hollywood Hills

**Pacific Design Center Extension**

The Pacific Design Center, or 'Blue Whale' was built in 1975 to house interior design showrooms. Its bright aquamarine colour, unusual form and drastic break in scale with the surrounding buildings aroused controversy. Designed as an object floating in space, it was never intended to be altered. So when asked to design an extension, Cesar Pelli & Associates decided to treat the original building as a single piece within a group of contrasting fragments.

This second phase consists of a bold, symmetrical element clad in green spandrel glass that rotates away from the original building but is connected to it via a two-storey blue plinth. Inside, 'Center Green' contains showrooms, a conference centre, a lecture hall, a three-level skylit atrium and a cylindrical escalator bank which will form the hinge to the third phase of development (more showrooms in a curved wedge clad in dark red glass).

Also included in the second phase is a parking structure for 1900 cars and a plaza which makes a grand urban space off San Vicente Boulevard at what was the back of the first building. On this plaza is an amphitheatre and the Murray Feldman Gallery, which is constructed in a contrasting poured-in-place concrete.

ADDRESS 8687 Melrose Avenue, West Hollywood 90069 [592–J7]
CLIENT Sequoia Pacific, Southern Pacific Company
ASSOCIATE ARCHITECTS Gruen Associates
STRUCTURAL ENGINEER Cygna Consulting Engineers
SIZE 470,000 square feet (43,600 square metres)
ACCESS open

**Cesar Pelli & Associates Inc 1988**

**Cesar Pelli & Associates Inc 1988**

**Center for Early Education**

Seen from nearby La Cienaga, this project, with its simple shapes, bulky massing, slender high tower and rooftops with security fences painted pastel green, looks like a Lego penitentiary. Disconcertingly attractive, it is as if the architecture of coercion had been rendered in Toy-Town form. Seen from Alfred Street, however, it becomes apparent that this is a school.

On a relatively small site, and with a modest budget, the architects have added a three-storey, 25,000-square-foot classroom building and underground garage to an existing two-storey brick structure. The slim tower houses an elevator and forms a focus for circulation. Open and enclosed stairs and bridges and a ground-level street provide access to the classrooms and the two rooftop playgrounds.

Although the old building has been extensively remodelled, the new building, parallel to Alfred Street, attracts most attention. Its bulk has been broken into two elements, one pink stuccoed, the other red, with a glass atrium between. A number of smaller pavilions are a further attempt to humanise the scale. A bus shelter with a hipped tin roof and cupola at the entrance makes reference to a country schoolhouse, while the pedimented arcade that fronts the new building evokes the classical tradition of learning.

An unplanned but appropriate mirror to the private CEE is the public (state) school opposite. PL

ADDRESS 563 North Alfred Street, West Hollywood 90048 [592-J7]
CLIENT Center for Early Education
STRUCTURAL ENGINEER Ismail & Otova
SIZE 67,000 square feet (6200 square metres)
COST $3.5 million
ACCESS none

**Goldman/Firth/Boccato Architects 1988**

**Goldman/Firth/Boccato Architects 1988**

**Propaganda Films**

Sandwiched between a stretch of Santa Monica Boulevard (noted for its transvestite prostitutes) to the north and a quiet residential area to the south, with a cement works to the west and the towering Bell and Howell records-storage building to the east, Propaganda Films is located in what you might call the 'real' Hollywood. The streets are lined with industrial buildings that cater to the film industry and through open doors one can glimpse treasure troves of lighting equipment and stage props.

Propaganda Films offers an unexpected cornucopia. Stepping inside the traditional bowstring-truss 1940s' warehouse, one sees what looks like the aftermath of a volcanic eruption. The middle of the building is filled by a large blue curved structure while smaller, odd shapes are scattered around it – the detritus, it seems, of some major upheaval.

Of course, it all makes sense. A complex programme – sound- and film-editing facilities, meeting rooms, offices, screening rooms, lounges, a casting room and a vault, among other things – has been conceptualised as an urban village. As in an exposed anthill, workspaces appear to be burrowed out of the different forms, while bridges and stairs climb and cross from place to place.

The architect best sums up the project when he says that the 'twin inspirations in form and mood were the movie set and a kind of cool, distant, alienation like that found in an Edward Hopper painting – a surrealistic vision of Los Angeles.' PL

ADDRESS 940 North Mansfield, Los Angeles 90038 [593–D7]
CLIENT Propaganda Films
STRUCTURAL ENGINEER Davis/Fejes
ACCESS none

**Franklin D Israel Design Associates Inc 1988**

West Hollywood/Hollywood/Hollywood Hills

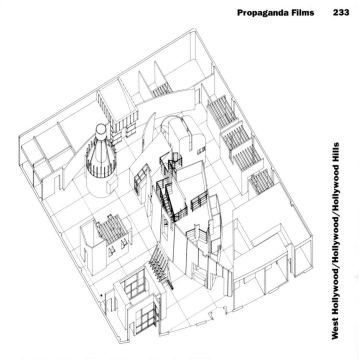

**Franklin D Israel Design Associates Inc 1988**

**Post Logic**

This remodel and expansion of a post-production company houses a new video-editing and film-transfer facility. The success of the scheme lies in the careful and inventive detailing that enlivens each room and corridor. The programme called for a reception area, machine room, two on-line video-editing bays, a video-graphics room and two telecine rooms.

The most arresting space is the reception area. Flying steel beams, shattered glass, red finply (a prefinished form-release plywood material imported from Finland) and the reception desk fill the area. The desk, built from black granite, maple cabinets, steel brackets and corrugated glass, is the focal element. It wraps itself around an existing building column and forms the corner between the two main access corridors to the studios.

In the corridors, as an alternative to acoustical tiles, wood panels in shard-like shapes are hung from the ceiling. This feature extends throughout the project, enlivening the hallways and adding interest to the long linear spaces.

The heart and brain of the project is the machine room which contains rows of the most advanced video and computer equipment displayed behind a custom-designed glass curtain wall. A window at the end of one of the corridors frames a close-up view of the Capitol Records building.

ADDRESS 1800 North Vine Street, Hollywood 90028 [593–F4]
CLIENT Miles Christensen
STRUCTURAL ENGINEERS Karl Frank and Constantine Tzantias
SIZE 6500 square feet (600 square metres)
COST $650,000
ACCESS lobby only

**studio bau:ton 1992**

West Hollywood/Hollywood/Hollywood Hills

**studio bau:ton 1992**

**Daniels Residence**

Jeffrey Daniels has built a carefully designed, light-filled tower for himself on a narrow, steeply sloping site in Laurel Canyon. Sophisticated spaces are stacked one over the other, with a double-height living area above the bedrooms which sit above a garage.

Gestures have been made in the elevations to unite the outside and inside. The front elevation uses verdigris copper fins reminiscent of those on the Kentucky Fried Chicken building (see page 216) while the rear elevation has an open-beamed canopy over the terrace.

West Hollywood/Hollywood/Hollywood Hills

ADDRESS 8617 Lookout Mountain Avenue, Los Angeles 90046 [592–J3]
CLIENT Jeffrey Daniels
STRUCTURAL ENGINEER Richard C C Lee
SIZE 2200 square feet (200 square metres)
ACCESS none

**Jeffrey Daniels & Associates 1992**

**Jeffrey Daniels & Associates 1992**

# Angélil/Graham Residence

This modestly sized house resting between a pair of retaining walls has a forceful presence. Situated on a steep site that appeared virtually unbuildable, a close collaboration between the architects and engineers resulted in an unorthodox strategy. Deep piles would have been the norm, but the architects opted instead for an unusual solution to stabilise the hill. Upper and lower retaining walls were built to create two garden levels linked by a grid of evenly spaced grade beams which forms a warped structural ladder.

The house is a simple double-height box which reads internally as a continuous space. Rooms are defined by sliding partitions and the second level is an open loft. Standard industrial materials are used throughout and large openings connect the inside and the outside.

The roughness of timber construction is paired with the sophistication of a steel system. The roof, supported by articulated steel beams balanced by tension wires, appear to float above walls clad in crude plywood siding. Continuous glazing between the roof and walls emphasises this separation and provides framed linear views of the hillside and the last rays of sunlight.

ADDRESS 6009 Rodgerton Drive, Los Angeles 90068 [593–F1]
CLIENT Marc Angélil and Sarah Graham
STRUCTURAL ENGINEER Ove Arup & Partners, California
SIZE 1800 square feet (170 square metres)
ACCESS none

**Angélil/Graham Architecture 1993**

**Angélil/Graham Architecture 1993**

# Dougherty/Ferange Residence

This is an extension and redesign of an existing house in the Hollywood Hills. Built on a steeply sloping site, the original two-storey structure has been expanded out towards the canyon and down two storeys. One enters at street level and immediately climbs the stair to the upper-level open-plan living area. Descending to the floor below street level, one enters a gallery to the cavernous double-volume master suite.

This house is full of wonderful details typical of Brian Murphy, with striking juxtaposition of an industrial aesthetic and a more polished finish. Small halogens hang from and plug into exposed conduits at ceiling level. Steel cross-bracings are exposed at the stairwell and against the double-height window in the master bedroom. The roof is a field of galvanised-steel skylight chambers with electric lights suspended over them to simulate a daylight effect at night. The landing and staircase treads are sandwiches of tempered and plate glass.

Hanging from a skylight into the void over the entry is a gold-leafed diamond-shaped panel of diamond-plate steel illuminated by a single halogen light – another Murphy chandelier? A surreal vignette is created where a square window with a view of the hillside across the street stands beside a photograph of the same view at the same scale.

The back elevation, which climbs down the canyon, can best be seen from Rising Glen Road.

ADDRESS 1885 Sunset Plaza Drive, Los Angeles 90069 [592–J4]
STRUCTURAL ENGINEER Joseph A Perazzelli
SIZE 3300 square feet (310 square metres)
COST $297,000
ACCESS none

**BAM Construction/Design Inc 1991**

**BAM Construction/Design Inc 1991**

**Prinster Residence**

Floating above the city, this house captures more than 180 degrees of spectacular Los Angeles view. Cavelike, it is closed at its back (which houses the entrance) and is completely glazed at its front to maximise the view.

Brian Murphy has a talent for transforming off-the-shelf products into things of unexpected beauty. Here, one enters through steel gates studded with clear glass marbles that refract the sunlight. The garage, which faces the street, is clad with corrugated-fibreglass panels that glow at night like 'the world's biggest lamp'.

Inside, the 18-foot-high living room is the major unifying space. To one side of it is the open dining area, which itself is open to the commercially fitted kitchen. To the other side is a media room whose enclosing wall is made from a series of frameless shopfront glass doors. A spiral stair climbs to a library mezzanine and a deck with views westward to the ocean. The mezzanine is constructed of expanded metal.

Walking past an open study/guest room, one arrives at the only enclosed space in the house – the master bedroom. The bed sits against a wall of translucent glass that separates the sleeping area from the open bathroom and storage. Another of the bathrooms has an amazing freestanding unit with a sculpted glass shower set at a 45-degree angle. On one side is a penitentiary-like stainless-steel toilet and on the other a spun stainless-steel washbasin with a convex traffic mirror hanging from copper pipes dropped from the ceiling.

ADDRESS 1641 Woods Drive, Los Angeles 90069 [593–A4]
CLIENT Patrick Prinster
STRUCTURAL ENGINEER Joseph A Perazzelli
SIZE 3000 square feet (280 square metres)
ACCESS none

**BAM Construction/Design Inc 1992**

**BAM Construction/Design Inc 1992**

# Goldberg-Bean Residence

A standard 1950s' ranch-style bungalow has been stretched to accommodate a new master-bedroom suite and study. In the process, it has metamorphosed from a mundane structure into what must be one of the most beautiful houses in LA.

On the street elevation, walls of yellow ochre stucco extend from the original structure towards a two-storey plywood box and a single-storey cube of concrete block. Beyond these, a plane of vivid cobalt blue stucco forces its way between two yellow layers.

From the garden, extensive glazing unites old and new and opens the house to the views over the scrubby wildness of Runyan Canyon. A steel-clad, curved element appears to be spiked to the ground by a tapering steel chimney. On the higher level, the ply box opens to a balcony that extends towards overhanging trees.

The complexity of the external massing belies the lucidity of the interior. Conventional room arrangements in the older part of the house give way to a freer flow of space in the new. A uniting force, hinted at on the exterior, is an undulating wall of colour-impregnated plaster that snakes its way sinuously through the house from the living area to the new master bathroom. The deepest of blues, it brings to mind the sculpture of Anish Kapoor. PL

ADDRESS 2029 Castilian Drive, Los Angeles 90068 [593–D2]
CLIENTS Howard Goldberg and Jim Bean
CONTRACTOR ART Construction
SIZE 4000 square feet (370 square metres)
ACCESS none

**Franklin D Israel Design Associates Inc 1992**

**Franklin D Israel Design Associates Inc 1992**

# Hollywood Duplex

These two strong, hard-edged boxes, simple and rigorous, extol the virtues of minimalism while using materials in a way that transmutes mundane concrete block, stucco and glass into something refined and unexpected.

The programme called for two separate structures on the steep, tightly v-shaped site. Excavation costs were kept to a minimum by making the basic footprint of each building as small as possible and letting each rise three storeys above garage/studio spaces. Behind the boxy fronts, volumes in the shape of piano-curves contain kitchens and bathrooms. Lodged in the space between the slightly skewed piano-curves and the boxes, stairways climb in appealing irregularity. Interiors are kept spartan in accordance with the loft ethos.

The severity of the exteriors is beginning to be softened as the gardens and trees establish themselves, but the Arab-influenced screened balconies remain too brutally free of creepers and the elegant proportions of the buildings cast a large shadow over their neighbours. PL

ADDRESS 6947–9 Camrose Drive, Los Angeles 90068 [593–D3]
CLIENT Ken Karswell
STRUCTURAL ENGINEER The Office of Gordon Polon
SIZE two 1650-square-foot (153-square-metre) units
COST $345,000
ACCESS none

**Koning Eizenberg Architecture 1987**

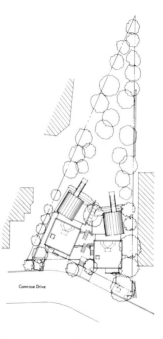

Camrose Drive

**Koning Eizenberg Architecture 1987**

# Silverlake/Echo Park/ Exposition Park/Downtown

# CDLT 1, 2 House

By replacing the familiar – fragments of walls and ceilings – and adding a 600-square-foot extension, Michael Rotondi has used his own house as a laboratory to work a bit of alchemy. While not producing gold itself, he has used steel, wood, plaster and concrete to create some powerful jewellery that suggests new ways of thinking about walls, windows, space, light and enclosure.

Rotondi describes his intentions and the process of this house's construction as follows:

'This house is a result of an interest in working full size, where the gap is closed between the moment of conception and the moment of occupation. Instead of it being a speculative act, the ideas came out of direct experience with the mind and body operating in the decision-making rather than just the mind. No working drawings were done for this project. Sketches were made for the contractor to work from each morning. At the end of the day the contractor would leave lights pointed at the areas that he had been working on that needed more work, or areas that were problems that needed to be resolved by the following morning.

'The way of working expanded and contracted simultaneously. The scale of the project and the fact of being one's own client made it possible to close the gap between idea and construction to ten minutes after a decision was made. Each component that was constructed would become the impetus for the next idea. Every layer was added to the next layer as opposed to intertwining them, and nothing was subtracted. The decision was made that no eraser would be used with this house, literally or figuratively. Instead of an idea merely feeding on itself as a kind of abstraction, the idea would be constructed, and the next idea came out of looking, or feeling on the skin the consequences of the previous decision.

'The builder had degrees in literature and music composition, so it was

**Michael Rotondi 1994**

**Michael Rotondi 1994**

possible to talk to him about things in a conceptual way that became a frame of reference for him to make decisions, trying to find a visual equivalent for musical concepts and notation. The house was intended to operate as a journal, to be a record of its own making and to somehow convey that it was made by another human being, as opposed to a machine, so there's conceptual fingerprints all over the building.'

ADDRESS 1955 Cedar Lodge Terrace, Silverlake 90039 [594–C4]
CLIENT Rotondi family
STRUCTURAL ENGINEER The Office of Gordon Polon
SIZE 600-square-foot (56-square-metre) addition to a remodelled 1200-square-foot (111-square-metre) house
ACCESS none

**Michael Rotondi 1994**

**Michael Rotondi 1994**

**California Aerospace Museum**

A Lockheed F-104 is caught in mid-flight and pinned to the wall above a 40-foot-high hangar door. A stucco box, a metal-clad polygon, a prism with a triangular and a sphere are placed in near collision to create a museum that celebrates an industry that has been a major force in Southern California.

Located in Exposition Park, a mall of sorts, the museum is surrounded by civic buildings including other museums, a sports arena, the Coliseum and a large rose garden and is sited so it can connect with the more classical armoury building. The entrance is in a passage between the two buildings. The interior has been designed as a single vast, hangar-like space with industrial-scale skylights and large windows that provide glimpses of the forms outside.

ADDRESS Exposition Park, 700 State Drive, Los Angeles 90037 [674-B2]
CLIENT California Office of the State Architect; Museum of Science and Industry
STRUCTURAL ENGINEER Kurily Szymanski Tchirkow
SIZE 28,000 square feet (2500 square metres)
COST $5 million
ACCESS open

**Frank O Gehry and Associates 1984**

**Frank O Gehry and Associates 1984**

**Loyola Law School**

Located in a rough area of downtown Los Angeles, the private Catholic institution wanted a campus that would be inwardly complex but would not overwhelm the surrounding neighbourhood, which is part of the Catholic Archdiocese. Gehry had a vision of the scheme as an acropolis or Roman Forum. This worked well with the clients' wish for a campus design that would refer to the ancient traditions and architecture of law.

What emerged is one of the most satisfying urban spaces in the city – a miniature piazza composed of three large buildings, four small buildings, sculpted green spaces and trees. The lecture halls are pulled out of the main building and placed around the site as single-room pavilions which though abstract are detailed in ways that evoke the past – Merrifield Hall has a pedimented roof and freestanding columns, Donovan Hall has a two-storey column-and-lintel façade, and the chapel a simplified Romanesque campanile. These are read against the brightly painted, rationally fenestrated wall of the Fritz B Burns Building, where the twisting stairways have been pulled outside to the front, with the central one capped by a grand pivoted greenhouse. In contrast to the horizontality of the Burns building is the more recent Cassasa Building, whose main façade is a brightly painted tower. This houses publications, law reviews and an extension to the library, which now resides in the renovated 1963 Law School.

Gehry has created a lively outside space. The ground level of the Burns Building addresses the piazza, with student offices, lounges, cafeteria and a bookstore opening on to a covered portico. Debates are held between the symbolic tree and the columns of Merrifield Hall and there is continuous movement on the exposed stairways.

Very little has been given to the surrounding streets. The backs and sides of the new buildings present inaccessible grey façades set behind a

**Frank O Gehry and Associates 1991**

continuous fence. Students and staff slip on to campus through the main Olympic Boulevard entrance, but they must have a security key. This is a scheme that keeps itself separate and secure from the possible danger of its neighbourhood. With its limited views of the city beyond the tops of its buildings, it feels like an oasis. The true gateway to the school is the nearly completed parking structure with its large articulated opening to the galvanised-metal façade facing the courtyard.

Merrifield Hall – pivoted 7° off grid – was to be the moot court where would-be lawyers practise the skill of oral argument in front of a panel of judges, but has been stripped of its symbolism now its function has been changed to a lecture hall.

ADDRESS 1441 West Olympic Boulevard, Los Angeles 90015 [634–C4]
CLIENT Loyola Marymount University
STRUCTURAL ENGINEERS Phases I and II: Johnson & Neilsen;
Phase III: Kurily Szymanski Tchirkow; Phase IV: Ove Arup & Partners, California
SIZE Phase I: 45,250 square feet (4200 square metres); Phase II: 8800 square feet (818 square metres); Phase III: 55,000 square feet (5100 square metres); Phase IV: 40,000 square feet (3700 square metres)
CONTRACT VALUE: Phase I: $3.6 million; Phase II: $957,000;
Phase III: $2.4 million; Phase IV: $6 million
ACCESS Monday to Friday 8.00–22.00; Saturday and Sunday 9.00–17.00

**Frank O Gehry and Associates 1991**

**Frank O Gehry and Associates 1991**

Arata Isozaki's first new building in the United States sits partially embedded in the parking structure for California Plaza, an 11.2-acre complex containing a hotel, retail space and commercial and residential towers. How did it get there? The law states that 1.5% of a commercial development's budget must be spent on public art, and while the California Plaza development was seeking planning approval the need for a museum of contemporary art in Los Angeles was being talked about. So the Community Redevelopment Agency instructed the developers to fulfil the public art requirement by financing a new museum.

The programme provides for galleries, an auditorium, a café, a bookstore, library, offices and a service area. The galleries are built one level below Grand Avenue and the service area below that. The forms visible at street level read as two separate volumes framing an open courtyard. This composition of solid and void expresses the Oriental philosophy of ying/yang. (It also satisfies the requirement to maintain both visual and physical connections to California Plaza's retail area.) Overlaid on this Oriental tradition is Isozaki's signature use of Platonic forms in an exuberant array of cube, cylinder and pyramids.

A deep, red Indian sandstone lends substance and a sense of monumentality. The light-heartedness of the post-modern cladding on the ticket cube and part of the administration building – aluminium panels painted green and laid in a diamond pattern with bright pink joints – provides a pleasing contrast.

To enter the museum, one descends to a sunken courtyard with a café on one side and a low-ceilinged entrance lobby on the other. The two gallery wings are proportioned according to the golden section and an anti-clockwise spiral leads through the seven exhibition spaces. Each space is distinctive in size, proportions and lighting,with three galleries

**Arata Isozaki & Associates 1986**

**Arata Isozaki & Associates 1986**

lit artificially and four naturally. Gallery A is the most dramatic space where a pyramidal, skylight-topped vault rises 60 feet above the floor. Throughout the gallery, skylights are made using the Oka-Lux system which diffuses light by sandwiching translucent glass and a layer of synthetic fibres between two layers of clear glass.

MOCA's other building, the Temporary Contemporary, is a masterful yet minimal intervention into a renovated police garage by Frank O Gehry and Associates (closed until 1995).

ADDRESS 250 South Grand Avenue, Los Angeles 90012 [634–F4]
CLIENT The Museum of Contemporary Art, Los Angeles
STRUCTURAL ENGINEER John A Martin & Associates
SIZE 98,000 square feet (9100 square metres)
COST $22 million
ACCESS Tuesday to Sunday, 11.00–17.00; Thursday, 11.00–20.00

**Arata Isozaki & Associates 1986**

**Arata Isozaki & Associates 1986**

# Genesis 1

Responding jointly of society and of the environment, Ted Hayes, founder and president of Justiceville/Homeless USA, has created a transitional community for homeless people. Situated in the shadow of the Harbor Freeway, it is made up of 20 semi-domed structures, or omnispheres, based on prototypes by Buckminster Fuller.

Each dome measures 20 feet in diameter and stands 12 feet high. Construction is from 21 bolted concave panels of non-toxic polyester fibre-glass with concrete pads as bases. The domes can be assembled in two hours by two people. Solar panels provide the lighting and should eventually generate enough power for all the utilities. The structures are now utilised privately as 1–2 person bedrooms and communally as kitchen, dining, workspace and bathrooms.

The occupants, described as 'Earthonauts' for inhabiting space-age technology on Earth, perform the necessary upkeep and will be taught work skills that could direct them towards self-sufficiency.

ADDRESS 847 Golden Avenue, Los Angeles 90017 [634–D4]
CLIENT Justiceville/Homeless USA
ASSOCIATE ARCHITECTS Jones and Martinez
SIZE 20 domes of 314 square feet (29 square metres) each
COST $6500 per dome
ACCESS site open

**Craig Chamberlain 1993**

**Craig Chamberlain 1993**

# Pershing Square

Exuberant colours, a delightful collection of spatial events and a perimeter sidewalk that re-establishes a connection with the surrounding urban fabric combine to make this new piazza one that might help restore Los Angeles' forgotten tradition of public spaces.

Pershing Square is the oldest public park in Los Angeles. Since its establishment in 1866 it has been renovated five times. In 1985 a competition to redesign the park was won by SITE and then abandoned when the association sponsoring it ceased to exist. Ricardo Legorreta and Hanna/Olin were approached by a new group, the Pershing Square Property Owners Association, but not commissioned until after the scheme had been approved by the community and by the city's various jurisdicial agencies.

The square sits on top of an underground parking lot built in 1950. The new design has created a sidewalk that circles the site and bridges the parking ramps to improve pedestrian access. Within the square are three buildings – a 120-foot-high purple tower and two yellow pavilions, one a police substation, the other a café.

A central axis running the length of the site plan is defined by three linear elements. Bordering 5th Street, a green area of raised terraces crowned by four majestic Canary Island palms will double as a stage for outdoor performances. Facing this is an amphitheatre of long low benches set on a carpet of grass. At its head is a circular, pebbled tidal pool fed by an aqueduct connected to the tower. The pool is capped by a curved concrete bench inscribed with a quotation from Carey McWilliams' book *Southern California Country*. The surface of the square is predominantly hardscape: courtyards, promenades and terraces are planted formally with several species of trees. The *Earthquake Line Fault* and telescopes that show earlier views of the square are by artist Barbara McCarren.

Making public spaces in the late 20th century has become a balancing

**Ricardo Legorreta and Hanna/Olin 1994**

**Ricardo Legorreta and Hanna/Olin 1994**

act between gestures to invite people in and attempts to control crime by limiting use. There, the café, food kiosks and public performances will tempt the community in. Intense lighting, clear sight lines, a minimum of grass and the absence of restrooms are intended to discourage crime and squatters. Hopes are high that the piazza will become an environment in which the presently fragmented ethnic and economic groups inhabiting the downtown area will mix.

ADDRESS block defined by 5th, 6th, South Hill and South Olive Streets, Los Angeles 900013 [634–E4]
CLIENT Pershing Square Property Owners Association acting on behalf of the City of Los Angeles
ASSOCIATE ARCHITECT Langdon Wilson Architecture and Planning
SIZE 5 acres (2 hectares)
COST $14.5 million
ACCESS open

**Ricardo Legorreta and Hanna/Olin 1994**

**Ricardo Legorreta and Hanna/Olin 1994**

**Gas Company Tower**

Under the guidance of (then) design-partner-in-charge Richard Keating and senior designer David Epstein, SOM has created a building that has almost instantly acquired the status of a landmark. If a straw poll and a few unsolicited comments are anything to go by, the Gas Company Tower is not only well known, but also well liked. And, apparently, most people know that the plan of the building's curved blue-glass crown mirrors the company's flame logo, which must please marketing gurus no end.

If people do complain, it is about the way this and the other towers made possible by the transfer of the Central Library's air rights to raise money for its extension (see page 274) overshadow the library itself. They could have a lot more to complain about. The 52-storey tower handles its 1.44 million square foot bulk with endearing lightness. SOM's facility with skins of glass and stone and the inspired way the more conventional volumes enclose the slippery blue glass, give the structure energy and movement. The fenestration, used to create perceptions of heaviness and lightness (and here SOM has learned well from New York's Chrysler Building), add to this buoyancy.

The tower's plinth at street level is less than exuberant, tending towards mausoleum sobriety, though on a difficult site that drops 60 feet and slopes in two directions this may be excusable. Attempts to enliven the base are too contrived to succeed. Shoji screens of rice paper laminated between glass tilt out from the office occupied by a Japanese bank, exhaust systems manifest themselves as large vents, but the overall effect is still gloomy.

To compensate for this, the tower has its own internal street with stores and a restaurant, and the building's two entrances are linked via terraces. The core of this space is a piazza where the elevator banks are massed. Here Italian Futurism elides with the sophistication of a late-1980s'

**Skidmore Owings & Merrill (Los Angeles) 1991**

Manhattan penthouse, arching spaces finished in precisely detailed stone, wood and steel. The limestone panels cladding the walls are hung from a steel framework without any jointing - allowing them to move independently in an earthquake and giving them a monumental quality. An almost seamless wall of glass looks out on to what could be the platforms of a 21st-century railway station, with rows of low fountains standing in for tracks and a block-long mural by Frank Stella that does something to alleviate the chilly exactness of the interior. PL

ADDRESS 555 West 5th Street, Los Angeles 90013 [634–E4]
CLIENT Maguire Thomas Partners
STRUCTURAL ENGINEERS CBM Engineers
SIZE 1.44 million square feet (134,000 square metres); 27,000 square foot (2500 square metres) floor plate
ACCESS lower levels are open during business hours

**Skidmore Owings & Merrill (Los Angeles) 1991**

**Skidmore Owings & Merrill (Los Angeles) 1991**

# Los Angeles Central Library Extension

Always a landmark, Los Angeles Central Library, designed by Bertram Goodhue and completed in 1926, is also a symbol of the city's moral health, of Downtown's regeneration and, now that it is surrounded by towering skyscrapers, of what has been lost.

Shaken by earthquakes and damaged by fire, the library has seemed to reflect the violent forces that have changed the economic and social landscape of Los Angeles over the last decade. Its symbolic power was evident in the large crowds that turned out to celebrate its reopening after five years of planning and six years of construction.

The original building – which Goodhue himself described as 'strange' – is a synthesis of modernity and antiquity that ends up as Mesopotamian fantasy. Strongly expressed masses climb like a truncated ziggurat to a tower topped by a tiled pyramid. Bas-relief and statuary enliven the concrete walls.

Adding a new wing to a structure so powerfully self-contained is no easy task and at best HHPA's Bradley Wing is nondescript. Lacking the forceful massing of the original, its energy is dissipated over a number of large, bland façades, somewhat ameliorated by the use of the architects' trademark glazed terra cotta

Entering through the old building, one is taken along low-ceilinged corridors that open in an unashamedly theatrical gesture on to the cathedral-sized atrium. Designed to bring light into the structure, this vast space runs the length of the wing, with the book stacks and reading rooms massed on either side.

With four floors above ground and four below, however – a fact made plain in the glazing of the far wall – one has the disconcerting feeling of being in a large elevator that is descending into the bowels of the earth. Reminiscent of the space HHPA created for the LACMA extension entry

**Hardy Holzman Pfeiffer Associates 1993**

**Hardy Holzman Pfeiffer Associates 1993**

stairway (see p 206), with massive glazed terra cotta columns lining one side like a Cecil B De Mille recreation of Babylon, the atrium is too high, too narrow, too big. It is an even greater anti-climax as one moves down on the escalators from level to level to … nothing very much. There are offices and book stacks, but in terms of movement through the building this is a dead-end and there is no choice but to retrace one's steps.

The fact that HHPA's drawings called for the bulk of the new wing to rise above ground and it was lowered only as the result of worries that it would overshadow Goodhue's building no doubt explains the feeling of a compromised design. By contrast, a visit to the library's rotunda, which Goodhue located beneath the tiled pyramid, provides a startling example of how manipulation of space can set one's spirit free.

Renovation of the library was largely paid for – there was a shortfall of some $80 million – by the sale of its air rights. This deal allowed the 77-storey First Interstate World Center, the 52-storey Gas Company Tower (see page 270), and the 40-storey 555 Hope Street building all to be erected nearby and to dwarf it. Symbolic again, one feels. PL

ADDRESS 630 West 5th Street, Los Angeles 90071 [634–E4]
CLIENT City of Los Angeles Board of Library Commissioners
STRUCTURAL ENGINEER Brandow and Johnston
SIZE 530,000 square feet (49,000 square metres)
COST $130 million (new wing and renovation)
ACCESS open

**Hardy Holzman Pfeiffer Associates 1993**

**Hardy Holzman Pfeiffer Associates 1993**

**Nicola**

This restaurant is located on the ground floor of the 72-storey Sanwa Bank Plaza. Partners Michael Rotondi and Clark Stevens have collaborated with Brian Reiff to create a dynamic environment that plays strongly on the theme of oppositions – the linear versus the curved, hard versus soft, man-made versus natural, open versus enclosed. The most arresting element is the ceiling, which is crowded with tightly spaced wooden ribs and curved metal tubes. The tubes provide a framework for bits of cut and twisted cloth that suggest a bank of cirrus clouds or a flock of birds. These swoop over the individual booths to light them with illuminated cloth cocoons.

Elsewhere, arched wooden ribs are used vertically as screens to define a more secluded seating area and to provide a veil for the kitchen. At times it seems as if the design has left little room for the people who use it, but this is easily forgiven because of its sheer beauty.

Another part of the restaurant occupies 900 square feet of the Sanwa Bank Plaza's six-storey skylit atrium. Bound by a screen of metal ribs stabilised by stone boulders, the lofty sensation of this space could not be more different from the enclosed atmosphere inside.

ADDRESS 601 South Figueroa Street, Los Angeles 90017 [634–D5]
CLIENT Larry Nicola
STRUCTURAL ENGINEER Joseph A Perazzelli
SIZE 1700 square feet (158 square metres) inside; 900 square feet (84 square metres) of terrace
ACCESS restaurant hours

**Roto NDI 1993**

**Roto NDI 1993**

**Broadway-Spring Center**

While there are a number of parks within the suburban sprawl of Los Angeles, public urban spaces are at a premium. When developers were seeking approval for an eleven-storey parking garage on a site bounded by the Bradbury building and land owned by the Community Redevelopment Agency, the CRA made a proviso before granting permission: if the developers would build and maintain a public urban space on its land, the project could go ahead.

This well-used space is dedicated to the African-American midwife Biddy Mason, who lived at 331 Spring Street from 1866 to 1891. Running along one side of the infill site is 3000 square feet of retail space accommodated in pavilion-like buildings. A water sculpture made up of a collection of metal tubes that play with water in different ways forms the focus of the landscape design.

ADDRESS 333 South Spring Street, Los Angeles 90013 [634–E5]
CLIENT Broadway-Spring Center Joint Venture
STRUCTURAL ENGINEER Freet, Yeh, Rosenbach
LANDSCAPE DESIGN Burton & Spitz
SIZE 3000 square feet (280 square metres) of building
COST $1.5 million
ACCESS open

**Office of Charles and Elizabeth Lee – Architects 1993**

**Office of Charles and Elizabeth Lee – Architects 1993**

# Los Angeles Convention Center Expansion Project

Designed to enlarge and modernise an existing facility that was feeling its age, Phase 1 of the Los Angeles Convention Center Expansion Project is seen as a crucial element in plans to regenerate Downtown and boost the local economy.

Gargantuan in scale, the new structures sit lightly at the south-western corner of Downtown, in the crook of the intersection of the Santa Monica and Harbor Freeways. The key element is the new main exhibition hall. Located south of the existing Convention Center and separated from it by Pico Boulevard, this vast space – 941 feet from end to end and 460 feet wide with 40-foot-high ceilings and 120-foot trusses that create 240-foot clear spans – is aligned on a diagonal to the orthogonal city grid. The decision to skew the axis created space in the north-east corner of the site for an entry lobby and made it possible to sweep the freeway-facing sides into one huge curve.

The main lobby is an 150-foot-high tower with glass walls covering a honeycomb of steel spars, its soaring light-filled space signifying the lofty ambitions of the project. A slightly smaller version of this tower provides a new entrance to the existing hall, and the two lobbies are linked by a glass-faced bridge of meeting rooms that spans Pico Boulevard. Thankfully, reflective glass was eschewed in favour of glass with a ceramic grid or frit baked into it. This dissipates the sun's heat and glare while allowing shadowy outlines of the structural-steel honeycomb to be seen from the outside and shafts of sunlight to penetrate the interior.

Inside the lobbies, Alexis Smith has created two terrazzo floor designs, one a projection of the Pacific Rim, the other of the night sky.. Matt Mullican has installed a series of friezes that explore subjects such as the

**Gruen Associates/Pei Cobb Freed & Partners 1993**

**Gruen Associates/Pei Cobb Freed & Partners 1993**

history of Southern California and the course of evolution.

Only the tops of the towers are visible from the freeway – like huge lightboxes above the sweeping curve of the loading bays. A wall of green-painted steel panels, this elevation addresses and mirrors the scale and flow of the freeway with the confidence of a giant billboard.

Taken on its own terms, the building is hard to fault. Carefully conceptualised, thoughtfully designed, exquisitely executed, it will no doubt make a good convention centre. Whether the lack of an integrated hotel – promised in Phase II – will seriously handicap it remains to be seen.

And yet …? Visiting the Convention Center raises questions. Like a Crystal Palace marking the end rather than the beginning of an era, it stands like a clean oil refinery or friendly nuclear power station in celebration of the technology, aesthetics and politics of an age already past. At a time when a lumbering brontosaurus of a building might have been more appropriate, it already seems a little forlorn. The unspoken irony of Mullican's evolutionary panels – that this is where we have been heading – might bring a smile to the lips of the Amway and Herbalife conventioneers. PL

ADDRESS 1201 South Figueroa Street, Los Angeles 90015 [634–D5]
CLIENT City of Los Angeles
STRUCTURAL ENGINEER John A Martin & Associates
SIZE 2,500,000 square feet (232,000 square metres)
COST $500 million (including site acquisition)
ACCESS open for conventions

**Gruen Associates/Pei Cobb Freed & Partners 1993**

**Silverlake/Echo Park/Exposition Park/Downtown**

**Gruen Associates/Pei Cobb Freed & Partners 1993**

# Simone Hotel

The Simone Hotel is a single-room occupancy (SRO) hotel in the 'Skid Row' area of Downtown. Its function is to provide affordable temporary accommodation for people who might otherwise be homeless. Commissioned by the Skid Row Housing Trust, the building had to be cheap and functional without being patronisingly institutional. Rooms are small but adequate. Bathrooms are shared on a ratio of one for every five rooms. Common rooms, including kitchens, lounges and laundry facilities, are located on the ground and fourth floors of the five-storey building, which means that they are no more than one floor away from any of the rooms.

Windows at the end of the corridors and a light-well bring natural light into the structure. Finishes are simple but more than merely functional, and the whole building has the well-scrubbed utilitarianism of a youth hostel.

The exterior is distinguished by a curved parapet, a band of glazing on the fourth floor and an arcaded ground level. PL

ADDRESS 520 San Julian Street, Los Angeles 90013 [634–E6]
CLIENT Skid Row Housing Trust
STRUCTURAL ENGINEERS Freet, Yeh, Rosenbach
SIZE 32,472 square feet (3000 square metres)
COST $3.9 million
ACCESS none

**Koning Eizenberg Architecture 1992**

**Koning Eizenberg Architecture 1992**

# Tarzana to Glendale

# Rice Residence

The Rice Residence is an odd interloper into the developer sprawl of the hills above Glendale. Cardboard mansions, no doubt billed as 'luxury estates', crowd the steeply climbing roads which force their way towards the mountains. Like a trip through time, one is taken to the absolute edge of the city, where development and nature collide and LA once again seems like a frontier town.

Ringed by such thin impersonations of the good life, it is as if the Rice Residence has been beamed in from another time and another continent. Japanese in its stoic imperturbability, its weighty concrete walls blankly face the street. The front door opens on to a small courtyard from which the main body of the house is entered. Divided into three distinct volumes, defined by their structural materials, the building steps back from the street and opens itself to the exceptional views. The concrete element gives way to a volume enclosed by double-height glass curtain walls that might seem more at home in a large commercial development. Freestanding stairs lead down to the living and kitchen areas or up to the master-bedroom suite which occupies the entire top floor of the third element in the design, a steel-framed and extensively glazed volume.

Monumental in its use of materials and its massing, the house is never-theless a welcoming family home. The quality of construction is outstanding. PL

ADDRESS 2096 Rimcrest Drive, Glendale 91202 [564–E1]
CLIENTS Chuck and Phyllis Rice
STRUCTURAL ENGINEER Stephen Perloff
SIZE 5900 square feet (550 square metres)
ACCESS none

**Lomax Rock Associates Architects 1993**

**Lomax Rock Associates Architects 1993**

# Team Disney Building

Don't be fooled. This building may introduce itself with slapstick humour, but apart from a few giggles inside, it takes itself and corporate architecture very seriously. This is one of three buildings built for the Walt Disney Company by Michael Graves – there are two hotels at Disney World in Orlando, Florida, the Dolphin and the Swan, which are most notable for the enormous sculptures (of dolphins and swans) that ornament them. This is by far the most restrained of the three.

With lower levels clad in red Indian sandstone and upper levels faced with a pale stucco, this building has examined its context and responded accordingly. The bulk of the L-shaped structure sits on the perimeter of the studio lot, absorbing the city grid and addressing the roads by providing edges to Alameda Avenue and Buena Vista Street. The corner is acknowledged and emphasised by additional ornament on the elevations, increased height and copper-clad vaulted roofs. The north part of the L connects to a six-storey cylindrical drum which allows the front block to rotate 20 degrees so that is in synch with the grid of the Disney lot (original streamline moderne buildings designed in 1939 by Kem Weber). Standing opposite a colonnaded reflecting pool is the classically inspired front elevation with 19-foot-tall replicas of the seven dwarves substituting as caryatids.

Once past this broad joke, things get earnest quickly as circulation is dictated by a formal procession of spaces. One passes through the foyer, an elevator lobby, and then enters the 25-foot-high rotunda. From here, one walks reverently through a long colonnaded courtyard into an oppressively dark atrium which connects to a second elevator lobby.

While this postmodern building never developes into more than a caricature, the suggestion of permanence is consistent throughout. In order to provide a ceiling inside that is clear of hardware and that can be read

**Michael Graves Architect 1991**

**Michael Graves Architect 1991**

as a simple plane, services are accommodated within the walls which gain a thickness that seems nearly ancient.

Throughout the interiors there has been a great deal of attention to detail, especially on the executive floors. Furniture is custom designed, producing a Mickey Mouse version of the Oculus chair and a conference table inlaid with tiny Mickeys. For the executive dining room on the top floor of the rotunda, Graves has designed the lighting, carpeting and china.

**Tarzana to Glendale**

ADDRESS 500 South Buena Vista Street, Burbank 91521 [563–F3]
CLIENT The Walt Disney Company
ASSOCIATE ARCHITECT Gruen Associates
STRUCTURAL ENGINEER John A Martin & Associates
SIZE 330,000 square feet (30,700 square metres)
ACCESS none

**Michael Graves Architect 1991**

**Michael Graves Architect 1991**

**Universal CityWalk**

Garish and over-designed like the other wildly successful commercial projects hatched from the same nest, this shopping mall impersonating a city street remains a shopping mall. John Jerde has long since established himself as the master of the mall and possesses considerable know-how when it comes to designing for mass appeal. Among his previous works are the Westside Pavilion in West Los Angeles, the unbelievably gaudy Horton Plaza in San Diego ('visual pollution', as one visitor remarked), and the more recent Treasure Island hotel and casino in Las Vegas.

Located at Universal Studios, these two blocks of restaurant and retail are hinged together by a large circular piazza covered by a space frame. Formally, this promenade serves to connect the Universal Studios tour and amphitheatre at one end with the 18-theatre multiplex cinema at the other. All the tenants have commissioned their own architects to design exteriors and interiors on the Jerde-provided shell. When it came to signage, the architects were informed that 'the only rule is that there are no rules'.

According to John Jerde, 'The style of Universal CityWalk architecture pays homage to Los Angeles, the theme of which is that there is no theme'. And so one gets a mixed bag of whimsy. Among the elevations are a 1957 Chevy crashing through a freeway sign that carries the name of an ice-cream shop and a spaceship that collides with the façade of a stockist of science-fiction comic books. Elsewhere, a shop selling beach clothes has a roof like a surfboard and a pool with miniature crashing waves. The elevations all along the street are adorned with unrelated, vintage neon signs advertising such things as motels and gasoline.

Writing in *LA Architect*, Steven Flusty described CityWalk thus: 'Godzilla, it would seem, had been busily grazing her way across the land-marks of the LA basin when, overcome by a chunk of Frederick's of Holly-

**The Jerde Partnership 1993**

wood caught in the back of her throat. she retched a stream of half-digested façades into Universal City's lap.'

Also occupying space in CityWalk is a UCLA satellite campus offering an extension programme that emphasises arts and entertainment. This exists as an attempt to tie CityWalk into the surrounding community. But it is in no physical way a continuation of the city – to access it one must navigate the physical barrier created by a confusing and expensive parking system.

This privatised, walled social area for the privileged has received a lot of criticism. While claiming to do so, it does not depict Los Angeles. Thanks to post-riot paranoia, it boasts very heavy security, no transients and no poor. Sinister.

ADDRESS 1000 Universal Center Drive, Universal City 91608 [563–C7]
CLIENT MCA Universal
EXECUTIVE ARCHITECT Daniel, Mann, Johnson & Mendenhall
SIZE 200,000 square feet (18,600 square metres)
ACCESS open

**The Jerde Partnership 1993**

**The Jerde Partnership 1993**

# DWP Van Nuys

The programme for a distribution HQ, administration and warehouse building for the Department of Water and Power could have resulted in a dreary set of buildings, but has instead yielded something both practical and attractive. A warehouse for tool storage and a low-lying office block pivot around a drum-shaped element that houses an assembly room. The warehouse, with its curved metal roof, seems like a section of an aircraft hanger. Its base of concrete block is topped by a thin band of small windows that alternate with stucco-work, with painted metal panels above.

The office block is more intimately scaled and dispenses with the industrial feel of the metal panels. The drum links these two forms physically and stylistically, with a crown of metal over stuccoed walls. A stairway leading to the second-floor entrance to the assembly room acknowledges the ceremonial functions of the building.

The sheds and car-parking structure that complete the site demonstrate the effectiveness of inspired restraint. While there is no bravura in this project, it nevertheless establishes a strong presence through thoughtful planning, appropriate use of materials and controlled detailing. Its northern-European feel brings to mind both Gunnar Asplund's Stockholm Public Library and, in the window treatments, the Dutch followers of Frank Lloyd Wright. PL

ADDRESS 14401 Saticoy Street, Van Nuys 91405 [532–A3]
CLIENT Department of Water and Power
STRUCTURAL ENGINEER Martin & Huang
SIZE 40,000 square feet (3700 square metres)
ACCESS none

**Ellerbe Becket 1992**

**Ellerbe Becket 1992**

# Shragg Residence

As in their own house (see page 50), Koning Eizenberg use open, external space to define the living areas of this residence. A two-storey volume containing most of the rooms runs along the northern edge of the lot, forming the backbone of the structure. To the east and west, single-storey elements – a garage closest to the street and a living area that opens on to the large garden – lie perpendicular to this axis, while between them a large, Barraganesque courtyard becomes the heart of the building.

The large suburban lot allowed the architects to spread out and explore the flow of spaces. Progression from street to motor court to courtyard to living area to garden is made smoothly, but with a dramatic highlight at each location: the ply-clad garage that recalls the early Californian Modernists; the sun-drenched courtyard that draws on the area's Mexican heritage; the Schindleresque fenestration of the stairway; the undulating roof of the living area – aptly described by the project architect as 'the magic carpet' – and the completely glazed east wall that looks out over the large garden.

The architects quote two maxims. One is Neutra's: a house is 'a machine in a garden.' The other is their own: 'A tree is as integral to our design as a wall or a roof.' PL

ADDRESS 6054 Calvin Avenue, Tarzana, 91356 [530–G7]
CLIENT Bruce Shragg
STRUCTURAL ENGINEER E Brad Graves
LANDSCAPE Robert Fletcher
SIZE 3000 square feet (280 square metres)
COST $448,000
ACCESS none

**Tarzana to Glendale**

**Koning Eizenberg Architecture 1992**

**Koning Eizenberg Architecture 1992**

# Index

Los Angeles: a guide to recent architecture

Los Angeles: a guide to recent architecture

*Los Angeles: a guide to recent architecture*

Los Angeles: a guide to recent architecture

Los Angeles: a guide to recent architecture

**Photographs**

The photographs on the pages listed here were taken by Erhard Pfeiffer whose work for this book is gratefully acknowledged: 4, 29, 31, 33, 35, 37, 51, 53, 55, 63, 69, 79, 83, 89, 91, 93, 95, 101, 103, 105, 107, 109, 111, 117, 119, 123, 127, 132, 133, 135, 137, 139, 143, 159, 161, 163, 165, 166, 173, 177, 185, 187, 189, 191, 195, 202, 203, 207, 209, 221, 241, 243, 245, 254, 255, 257, 259, 261, 263, 265, 267, 269, 271, 273, 275, 277, 281, 283, 285, 297, 298, 299, 301, 303

Other photographs were taken by:
Peter Whiteley, page 41
Julius Shulman, pages 45, 239
Ron Pollard, pages 61, 213
Tim Street-Porter, page 77
Chris Dow, page 97
Greg Crawford, pages 99, 154
Grant Mudford, pages 115, 217
Tom Bonner, pages 149, 199, 229
Paul Warchol, pages 182, 183
Tim Hursley, page 193
Foaad Farah, page 211
J Scott Smith, page 215
Mark Lohman, page 223
Douglas Hill, pages 236, 237
Hewitt/Garrison, page 287